SONIC UNLEASHED™

PRIMA Official Game Guide

Written by:

OffBase Productions

Prima Games

An Imprint of Random House, Inc.

3000 Lava Ridge Court, Suite 100
Roseville, CA 95661
www.primagames.com

Acknowledgements:

Special thanks to Kristin Parcell, Cindy Chau, Kevin Frane, Patrick Riley, Hiroshi Seno, and Judy Gilbertson.

ISBN: 978-0-7615-6000-5
Library of Congress Catalog Card Number: 2008927758
Printed in the United States of America

08 09 10 11 LL 10 9 8 7 6 5 4 3 2 1

D1228062

Contents

INTRODUCTION

Sonic's never-ending battle against his nemesis, Dr. Eggman, has led him to the mad scientist's battle fleet floating ominously in the stratosphere. Blazing a destructive path to the central fortress where Eggman is holed up, Sonic transforms into Super Sonic, harnessing the power of the Chaos Emeralds. Unfortunately, his amazing powers are not enough to defeat the madman, and he finds himself the victim of another one of Eggman's nefarious traps.

Surrounded and blasted by an energy shield, Sonic is stripped of his Super Sonic powers and robbed of the Chaos Emeralds, whose energy is used to fire a powerful beam toward the world below. With a deafening roar, the world is ripped into seven continents, exposing its molten core underneath and awakening a colossal beast—Dark Gaia—from its long slumber. Eggman had planned all along to exploit Dark Gaia as a means of taking over the world.

However, Dark Gaia is not the only beast unleashed this day. Due to his close proximity to the Chaos Emeralds as the dark energy is expelled, Sonic undergoes a harsh transformation. His muscular density is increased, his claws are sharpened, his teeth grow into fangs, and his body becomes covered with fur. Sonic the Werehog is now unleashed.

It's up to Sonic to come to grips with his mysterious transformation, figure out a way to restore the continents of the planet, and take down Eggman once and for all in the most fierce and deadly battle of his life.

SONIC
UNLEASHED™

CHARACTERS UNLEASHED

Sonic the Hedgehog

Sonic is the world's fastest supersonic hedgehog who values freedom and living his life by his own rules. Champion of those who can't defend themselves, he is kind at heart but can also be short-tempered, thus earning the nickname "Blue Dude with a 'Tude." Quick to throw himself into the middle of trouble without a second thought, Sonic always remains steadfast to the very end. His personality is a combination of kindness and ferocity, as he does all in his power to snuff out evil, but he also can't look away when somebody else is in trouble. Sonic hates boredom and being tied down, so he spends much of his time running toward danger or the next adventure.

Sonic the Werehog

An unintentional result of Dr. Eggman's latest assault on the blue hedgehog, Sonic now undergoes an extreme physical transformation whenever the sun goes down, but thankfully his heart and demeanor remain the same...well, almost. Known as Sonic the Werehog, this beefier, harrier, slower, and tougher version is still willing to put his life on the line for his friends. But his dedication to helping his new friend Chip regain his memory is partly out of guilt, because it was his own fall from space after Eggman's attack that caused Chip's amnesia in the first place. As a Werehog, Sonic is not as fast as his usual self, but he makes up for it with ferocious, melee-style combat techniques. His powerful arms are able to stretch, allowing him to attack enemies from a greater distance and to reach distant ledges, poles, and bars with ease.

SONIC UNLEASHED™

Chip

Poor Chip. Talk about being in the wrong place at the wrong time. This little creature lost his memory after Sonic's free fall from outer space. Since he no longer knows who he is or where he came from, Chip decides to join Sonic on his world adventure in an effort to try to rediscover his identity. During the trek, Chip also serves as a guide, giving Sonic various tips and hints along the way.

Tails

His real name is "Miles Tails Prower," but his friends just call him "Tails." He's a little kid fox with two tails that he uses to temporarily fly and hover in the air. Friendly and with a heart of gold, Tails considers Sonic his best pal and loves tinkering with machinery. He also is a crack pilot and can fly Sonic around the world on his biplane, the Tornado.

Amy

Sonic's self-proclaimed girlfriend, Amy Rose, has been chasing the blue hero and trying to win his heart ever since she first met him. Having been involved in many of Sonic's adventures, Amy is very familiar with Dr. Eggman and his nefarious plots (sometimes getting mixed up right in the middle of them). This time around, she has no idea that the blue behemoth that is Sonic the Werehog is actually her beloved.

Dr. Eggman (aka Dr. Robotnik)

The long-suffering archenemy of Sonic, Dr. Eggman is an evil scientific genius who boasts an IQ of 300. While he never has been able to best Sonic, he never gives up trying. This time around, by skillfully luring the speedy hedgehog right into his most devious traps, he has been able to successfully awaken Dark Gaia. But will he be equally successful in taking over the world once and for all?

SONIC UNLEASHED™

GETTING UP TO SPEED
Controls

WII REMOTE™ AND NUNCHUK™	
Menu Controls	
Make Selection	Pointer/Control Stick/+Control Pad
Accept	Ⓐ
Cancel	Ⓑ
Pause Menu	⊕
Sonic the Hedgehog Controls	
Move/Brake	◎
Quick Step	Hold Ⓑ and ◎ left or right
Quick Jump/Spin Attack	Ⓐ
Wall Jump	◎ and Ⓐ
Crouch/Slide	Ⓩ
Sonic Drift	◎ left or right and Ⓩ
Homing Attack	Shake the Wii Remote™ while in the air
Lightspeed Dash	Shake the Wii Remote™
Sonic Boost	Shake the Wii Remote™
Stomping	Ⓑ or Ⓩ while jumping
Sonic the Werehog Controls	
Move/Dash	◎
Jump	Ⓐ
Guarding	Ⓩ
Right-Handed Attack	Shake the Wii Remote™
Left-Handed Attack	Shake the Nunchuk™
Two Handed Attack	Shake both the Wii Remote™ and Nunchuk™
Dash Attack	◎ and Shake the Wii Remote™ or Shake the Nunchuk™
Combos	Shake the Wii Remote™ and Nunchuk™ alternately
Grab	Ⓑ
Throw	Shake the Wii Remote™ while grabbing
Unleashed Mode	Ⓒ
Spinning Poles	Move Wii Remote™ in circular motion
Opening Doors	Swing both the Wii Remote™ and Nunchuk™ upwards
Move Lever	Swing the Wii Remote™ from left to right
Turning Cranks	Ⓑ and rotate ◎

CLASSIC CONTROLLER	
Menu Controls	
Make Selection	L Stick
Accept	a Button
Cancel	b Button
Pause Menu	+/START Button
Sonic the Hedgehog Controls	
Move/Brake	L Stick
Quick Step	L Button/R Button
Quick Jump/Spin Attack	b Button
Wall Jump	b Button and L Stick left or right
Crouch/Slide	y Button
Sonic Drift	y Button and L Stick left or right
Homing Attack	b Button/x Button
Lightspeed Dash	x Button
Sonic Boost	x Button
Stomping	y Button
Sonic the Werehog Controls	
Move/Dash	L Stick
Jump	b Button
Guarding	L Button
Right-Handed Attack	y Button
Left-Handed Attack	x Button
Two Handed Attack	a Button
Combos	x Button and y Button alternately
Grab	R Button
Throw	b Button while grabbing
Unleashed Mode	ZL Button/ZR Button
Spinning Poles	L Stick to start spinning
Opening Doors	R Button
Move Lever	R Button
Turning Cranks	L Stick

NINTENDO GAMECUBE CONTROLLER

Menu Controls

Make Selection	◎
Accept	Ⓐ
Cancel	Ⓑ
Pause Menu	START

Sonic the Hedgehog Controls

Move/Brake	◎
Quick Step	L / R
Quick Jump/Spin Attack	Ⓐ
Wall Jump	Ⓐ and ◎ left or right
Crouch/Slide	Ⓑ
Sonic Drift	Ⓑ and ◎ left or right
Homing Attack	Ⓐ/Ⓧ/Ⓨ
Lightspeed Dash	Ⓧ/Ⓨ
Sonic Boost	Ⓨ
Stomping	Ⓑ

Sonic the Werehog Controls

Move/Dash	◎
Jump	Ⓐ
Guarding	Ⓑ
Right-Handed Attack	R
Left-Handed Attack	L
Two Handed Attack	L and R
Combos	L and R alternately
Grab	Ⓧ
Throw	Ⓐ while grabbing
Unleashed Mode	Ⓨ
Spinning Poles	◎ to start spinning
Opening Doors	Ⓧ
Move Lever	Ⓧ
Turning Cranks	◎

DUALSHOCK®2 ANALOG CONTROLLER

Menu Controls

Make Selection	Directional Buttons
Accept	✕
Cancel	●
Pause Menu	START

Sonic the Hedgehog Controls

Move/Brake	ANALOG
Quick Step	L1 / R1
Quick Jump/Spin Attack	✕
Wall Jump	✕ and ANALOG left or right
Crouch/Slide	■
Sonic Drift	■ and ANALOG stick left or right
Homing Attack	✕
Lightspeed Dash	●
Sonic Boost	●
Stomping	■

Sonic the Werehog Controls

Move/Dash	ANALOG
Jump	✕
Guarding	L1
Right-Handed Attack	●
Left-Handed Attack	■
Two Handed Attack	✕
Combos	● and ■ alternately
Grab	R1
Throw	✕ while grabbing
Unleashed Mode	L1 + R1
Spinning Poles	ANALOG
Opening Doors	R1
Move Lever	R1
Turning Cranks	ANALOG

GAME SCREEN

Daytime

Lives Remaining

The Sonic icon counts down your remaining lives. This is shown in required missions only.

Target Time

This shows the target time Sonic must strive to complete his mission by. This is shown in required missions only.

Elapsed Time

The Clock icon counts the time Sonic has spent on his mission. This is shown in required missions only.

Rings in Possession

The number next to the Ring icon indicates how many rings Sonic has collected.

Boost Gauge

The gauge next to the Ring icon is the Boost Gauge. When a bar is filled, Sonic can perform a Sonic Boost.

Time Remaining

This Clock icon lets you know how much time Sonic has left to complete his mission or reach the next checkpoint. This is shown only in some optional missions and secret missions.

Rings Collected and Needed

This counter informs you of how many rings you have collected and how many more are needed to complete the mission. This is shown only in some optional and secret missions.

Nighttime

Lives Remaining

The Sonic the Werehog icon counts down your remaining lives.

Elapsed Time

The Clock icon counts the time Sonic the Werehog has spent on his mission.

Life Gauge

The green Life Gauge displays the amount of remaining health.

Unleashed Gauge

The Unleashed Gauge, located under the Life Gauge, displays Sonic the Werehog's Unleashed power.

Combo Count

This counter lets you know how many attacks you have successfully strung together.

Short-Range Map

The Short-Range Map gives you a overview of your surrounding area.

Boss Stages

Lives Remaining

The Sonic icon counts down your remaining lives.

Target Time for a Medal

This is the target time Sonic aims for to get a Sun or Moon Medal.

Elapsed Time

The counting clock shows how much time has passed since Sonic began the stage.

Boss's Vitality Gauge

The gauge at the top shows how much of the boss's health remains.

Life Gauge

The green Life Gauge displays the amount of remaining health. This is only for nighttime bosses.

Unleashed Gauge

The Unleashed Gauge, located under the Life Gauge, displays Sonic the Werehog's Unleashed power. This is only for nighttime bosses.

Rings in Possession

The number next to the Ring icon indicates how many rings Sonic has collected. This is only for daytime bosses.

Boost Gauge

The gauge next to the Ring icon is the Boost Gauge. When a bar is filled, Sonic can perform a Sonic Boost. This is only for daytime bosses.

Gaia Gate

Number of Sun Medals

The number next to the Sun Medals icon indicates how many Sun Medals you have.

Number of Moon Medals

The number next to the Moon Medals icon indicates how many Moon Medals you have.

Life Gauge

The green Life Gauge displays the amount of remaining health. This displays when Sonic is a Werehog.

Unleashed Gauge

The Unleashed Gauge, located under the Life Gauge, displays Sonic the Werehog's Unleashed power. This displays when Sonic is a Werehog.

Rings in Possession

The number next to the Ring icon indicates how many rings Sonic has collected. This displays when Sonic is a Hedgehog.

Boost Gauge

The gauge next to the Ring icon is the Boost Gauge. When a bar is filled, Sonic can perform a Sonic Boost. This displays when Sonic is a Hedgehog.

Results Screen (Daytime)

Chapter Times

These indicate what time you received for each of the mission's sections.

Rank

This shows the rank you earned from the mission. Earning an S grants you three Moon Medals, an A grants you two Moon Medals, a B grants you one Moon Medal, and a C grants you no medals. Clearing submissions grants you one Moon Medal.

Results Screen (Nighttime)

Record Time

Defeat the record time to increase your rank.

Rings

Collect more than the set amount to raise your rank even higher!

Force Collected

Gain more than the set amount of red orbs to beef up your rank!

Orb Results Screen (Nighttime)

This screen appears after the Results screen for the Nighttime stages. The orb results display how many red orbs you collected in the most recently completed stage. As these orbs accumulate your Vitality, Combat, or Attack Power rank may increase or you may learn a new attack skill.

MENUS
Main Menu

During the opening movie, press ⊕ (⊕/START for the classic controller or (START) for the GameCube controller) to access the Main menu. Navigate the menu with the pointer, control stick or control pad to move between the two options. (Use the L stick for the classic controller or the control stick for the GameCube.)

Select "Start Game" to begin your adventure with Sonic or choose "Options" to access the Options menu.

Pause Menu

During the stages or inside Gaia Gate, press ⊕ (⊕/START for the classic controller or (START) for the GameCube to access the Pause menu. Move through the menu's three options. Accept an option with on any controller. To cancel, press ® on any controller; press the button again to close the Pause menu.

Select "Continue" to return to your game. Choose "Restart Stage" to try the current stage again from the beginning. Selecting "Return to World Map" brings you back to the world map.

World Map

Number of Lives to Start Required Missions

The Sonic icon counts down your remaining lives.

Number of Sun Medals

The number next to the Sun Medals icon indicates how many Sun Medals you have.

Number of Moon Medals

The number next to the Moon Medals icon indicates how many Moon Medals you have.

Name of the Area

Here you can see the name of the highlighted location.

Change Menu

Use ⊕ or ⊖ (L or R for the Classic and GameCube controllers, respectively) to move between menus.

Your Next Destination

The world map appears after completing the first area of the game. On the map are the different locations you can travel to. Hold Z and use the control stick to rotate the world (use the L stick for the Classic Controller or the control stick for the GameCube). To select a location, use the pointer or the control pad for the classic and GameCube controllers. You can also change to the Overall Status and Extras screens using ⊕ or ⊖ (L or R for the Classic and GameCube controllers, respectively).

Villages

Local Destinations

These are the places you can travel to within the village.

Change Time

Select this icon to switch between day and night. This option may not be available right away.

Return to World Map

Once the world map is available, you can select this option to return to it.

Your Next Destination

This is the name of your next destination.

GAME ELEMENTS AND ITEMS

Grind Rail

Jump on and use these to zip through the stage.

Dash Panel

Run over this panel to be launched full speed in the direction of the panel's arrows. Get ready to feel the wind in your spikes!

Speed Ring

Pass through a speed ring to be sent through the air.

Springs

All it takes is one touch and Sonic is bounced in the spring's set direction. Springs are sometimes Homing Attack targets.

Item Capsules

Collect these capsules to gain special items found on the world map's Extras screen.

Ramp

Zoom over this object to be sent flying into the air.

Switch

Step on one to find out what it does!

Secret Mission Keys

Collect these rare keys to unlock a secret mission!

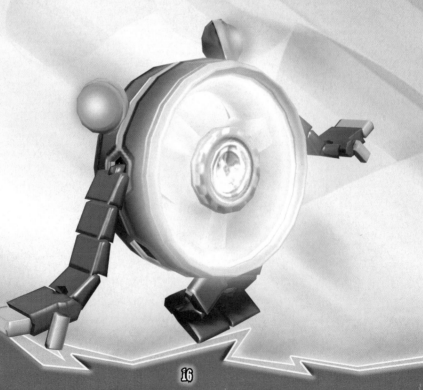

Rings

Collect rings to fulfill mission requirements and protect your hide! If you take damage without any rings in your possession, it's lights out. Some rings are larger and contain a number that stands for how many rings you gain by collecting that one.

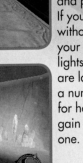

Orbs

Orbs are located inside some item capsules and in nighttime stages. Green orbs restore the Life Gauge, blue orbs fill the Unleashed Gauge, and red orbs give you experience points.

Level-Up

At the beginning of daytime stages, Sonic starts with three empty units in the Boost Gauge. You can fill the gauge with rings, Action Chains, and Drift Bonuses. Collecting more than the necessary rings, Action Chains, or Drift Bonuses results in a level-up, adding a unit to the Boost Gauge.

Were-Wallop

As a Werehog, Sonic gains experience points by collecting red orbs from certain item capsules. With enough experience points, you can learn the Were-Wallop skill. The Were-Wallop Combo, when used successfully, sends enemies flying. It is an excellent combo starter.

ADVANCED MOVES AND ATTACKS

Actions Chains

Connecting a series of Homing Attacks on enemies, obstacles, or objects results in Action Chains. These will fill the Boost Gauge before you know it! This is only available during daytime stages.

RESTORING THE FIRST CONTINENT
Apotos

This is a quaint seaside village lined with cobblestone streets and renowned for its lighthouse, windmills, and chocolate chip sundaes

VILLAGE: DAYTIME

Location	Name	Description	Unlocks	Rewards
Flower Street	Alexis	A young boy who suggests Sonic and Chip seek out the priest Gregorios	—	—
Cafe Terrace	N/A	Uninhabited during the day	—	—
Bell Square	Lambros and Eric	Kindly gents who haven't seen Chip before	—	Revisit them to obtain Secret Soundtrack 32
Windmill Coast Street	Gregorios	A wizened old priest who is fearful for the town's survival after the earthquake	Sacred Shrine	—
Sacred Shrine	—	A sacred place at the edge of town	Daytime missions	First continent's Sun Tablet (gift from Chip)

Sonic lands uncomfortably but unhurt just outside the village of Apotos, where he makes the acquaintance of a strange little creature who has lost his memory.

The odd couple decides to seek answers in the nearby village about the little fella's identity and about Sonic's transformation. On the way, Sonic will need to practice some of his basic skills.

Run forward and take advantage of Sonic's leaping ability to make it to the Goal Ring. Just three easy hops and you're there.

Required Missions

USE JUMPS TO REACH THE GOAL RING!

Type	Reward(s)	Items Found	Unlocks
Daytime	Moon Medal	—	Use the Sonic Drift on turns!

The first of the tutorial stages, this mission requires jumping to reach the Goal Ring.

USE THE SONIC DRIFT ON TURNS!

Type	Reward(s)	Items Found	Unlocks
Daytime	Moon Medal	—	Chain Homing Attacks together

The second of the tutorial stages, this mission teaches you the usefulness of drifting.

Drift through the switchback and hit the dash panels.

CHAIN HOMING ATTACKS TOGETHER!

Type	Reward(s)	Items Found	Unlocks
Daytime	Moon Medal	—	Blast off with a Sonic Boost!

The third tutorial stage imparts the effectiveness of Homing Attacks.

SONIC UNLEASHED™

Run forward and hit the springs to send Sonic high into the air. Sonic automatically targets the nearby enemy, so follow the onscreen prompts to attack and destroy the foe in midair. While still airborne, attack the next enemy in line. Once you land, head for the Goal Ring to finish the stage.

NOTE

Chaining two or more Homing Attacks together is called an Action Chain. Performing Action Chains rapidly fills up Sonic's Boost Gauge.

BLAST OFF WITH A SONIC BOOST!

Type	Reward(s)	Items Found	Unlocks
Daytime	Moon Medal	—	Slip under obstacles by sliding!

The fourth tutorial stage illustrates how to use Sonic's speed as a weapon.

Run straight ahead and pick up at least 14 of the rings that sit in the middle of the street. This will fill your Boost Gauge just enough to perform one Sonic Boost. As you approach the group of enemies, execute a Sonic Boost and run directly through them; your momentum will send them flying and give you a clear shot at the Goal Ring.

SLIP UNDER OBSTACLES BY SLIDING!

Type	Reward(s)	Items Found	Unlocks
Daytime	Moon Medal	—	Dodge on a dime with a Quick Step!

Tight squeezes are no problem after you learn how to slide under low-hanging obstacles.

Run forward and slide beneath the wall to retain your speed on the other side. Hit the Goal Ring running to put an end to this slick mission.

DODGE ON A DIME WITH A QUICK STEP!

Type	Reward(s)	Items Found	Unlocks
Daytime	Moon Medal	—	Head for the Goal Ring 1

Dodging enemies and quickly sidestepping to a more advantageous position is no problem with Sonic's Quick Step.

Three pairs of enemies await your arrival on this long, straight stretch of road. Quick Step between or around them to reach the Goal Ring none the worse for wear.

CAUTION

After completing this mission, you'll be asked if you want to continue. Selecting "No" will end your session and send you to the title screen. Select "Yes" to continue to the next required mission.

HEAD FOR THE GOAL RING 1

Type	Reward(s)	Items Found	Unlocks
Daytime	Moon Medal	Secret Document 3, Secret Illustration 57, Secret Move 1	Head for the Goal Ring 2

Time	Ranking	Reward
1'10'000	S	Three Moon Medals
1'20'000	A	Two Moon Medals
2'00'000	B	One Moon Medal

Utilize all that you've learned to reach the Goal Ring as quickly as you can.

The first straightaway is all about collecting rings. Stick to the center of the road and grab them all.

Boost through the remainder of the straightaway and drift around the corner, hitting the dash panel that sits in the path's center. A second dash panel sits on the path's left, around the next corner. Hit it and

more rings are yours for the grabbing. If you miss it, use a Sonic Boost to quicken your trip down the long road.

A raised dash panel fires Sonic off the cliff's edge, allowing him to sail through a red ring and reach 10 gold rings. Once you touch down, stay to the path's middle and connect with two more dash panels.

Hit the spring at the end of the dirt path and you'll be flung high into the air. Sonic will auto-target a robot standing on an elevated walkway. Perform a Homing Attack to defeat the enemy and reach the walkway. You'll land on a dash panel, which will send you speeding along. Be careful not to lose your footing while navigating the left turn, and aim for the dash panel on the walkway's left. Another spring will send you through a red ring, allowing you to bypass the enemies below.

Item!

Grab this item that sits in the center of the elevated walkway.

Travel down the path, using Sonic Boosts to retain speed and hit the dash panel at the narrow-tunnel entrance. The spring at the tunnel's exit sends you flyin'. Chain three Homing Attacks together to eliminate the hovering enemies and to expedite your passage through the valley.

Use the power stored in your Boost Gauge to keep up your speed as you navigate the bendy road. A dash panel sits on the path's left, after you make a slight right turn. This will give

you all the momentum you need in order to drift around the upcoming hairpin turn. After the turn, stick to the road's center to pick up more rings and to ensure you hit the upcoming rais dash panel.

Boost just before hitting th raised dash panel to make it through a red ring that sends you speeding towar a couple of strategically placed springs. If you hit the red ring, there's nothin to do but enjoy the ride. A rainbow ring will send you spiraling toward a long line of ring perfect for refilling your Boost Gauge.

Item!

Grab this item at the end of the line of rings.

Once you land on Apotos' cobblestoned streets, keep straight or risk colliding wi the houses on either side o the narrow thoroughfare. A dead end approaches quickly; slide beneath the wall and continue through the town. Take a hard right and you'll have a choice of paths. Take the right path, which slopes gradually upward. Stick to th dead center of the road to grab rings and an item, and to hit the dash panel.

Item!

Choose the right path at the split to grab this item.

Once you land, boost your way to the Goal Ring.

Apotos holds many curiosities for Sonic's small companion, not the least of which are its ice-cream sundaes. It appears the little guy has a large sweet tooth! Sonic names his traveling companion Chip because of his love for everything chocolate.

Talk to Alexis on Flower Street, who refers you to Gregorios. Eager for answers, speak to Gregorios on Windmill Coast Street and ask him for directions to the Sacred Shrine. On your way to the shrine, Chip gives you the first continent's Sun Tablet, which will open the Sun Door and allow you to complete additional required missions.

Item!

After speaking to Gregorios, be sure to revisit Eric on Bell Street to obtain Secret Soundtrack 32.

Required Missions

HEAD FOR THE GOAL RING 2

Type	Reward(s)	Items Found	Unlocks
Daytime	Moon Medal	Secret Illustration 4, Secret Document 17, Secret Document 20, Secret Illustration 32	Gather rings at top speed!

Time	Ranking	Reward
3'50'000	S	Three Moon Medals
4'20'000	A	Two Moon Medals
2'??'000	B	One Moon Medal

Utilize all that you've learned to reach the Goal Ring as quickly as you can.

Stick to the center of the street to pick up several rings. You'll gradually gain speed as you travel; don't lose it as you navigate the first two turns. After the second turn, hit the dash panel located in the street's center to pick up an adequate number of rings; this partially fills your Boost Gauge.

Boost through the tunnel and unleash a Homing Attack on the enemy waiting for you at the exit. Quickly perform a second Homing Attack to reach a narrow, elevated catwalk. One final Homing Attack on a spring will send Sonic flying across to the street's upper level.

A dash panel will send you zooming toward a fork in the path. Stick to the right; it's a much shorter and faster route. Race down the narrow path, hitting the dash panel and picking up the item along the way. The path veers sharply to the left; resist boosting as you approach it or you'll fly off the high path. Instead, hug the left wall and hit the spring located at the walkway's end; this launches you onto a narrow awning. Run down the awning and hop through the rainbow ring to propel Sonic through the air.

Item!

This item sits on a narrow path—easy pickings as you race by.

After you exit a small tunnel, prepare to enjoy some classic side-scrolling action. Boost down the path and jump onto an elevated porch. Use a Homing Attack to quickly reach a spring and launch onto the rooftops. Complete a loop at top speed and you'll be launched onto a rail to enjoy some hedgehog grinding.

Once you land, slide beneath two narrow openings, and a dash panel pad will propel you into a spring. Perform three Homing Attacks and you'll reach another rail. At the rail's end, another spring fires Sonic toward three more stationary robots. Once the first is auto-targeted, perform a Homing Attack to turn it into scrap. Quickly pull off three more attacks to finish the other two robots and to grab a zip line.

Boost atop the blue walkway to reach the bottom of the windmill as quickly as possible. Hit the raised dash panel and follow the onscreen prompts. Successfully hit all three buttons when prompted to leap to an elevated walkway. Boost through the straightaway, picking up an item as you go. Jump just before you reach the path's end to leap through the two red rings and the rainbow ring. Once you hit the ground, boost through the three robot enemies.

Item!

Successfully follow the onscreen button presses to reach the elevated walkway and this item.

After knocking the three robots off their feet, settle in for a long sprint. Use the dash panels and Sonic Boosts to make the best time. Once you enter the village, drift around a hard left turn and connect with a spring at the road's end. Chain two Homing Attacks together to reach the rainbow ring and avoid the lower path.

Boost along another street and drift to the right just before the road makes a sharp right turn. To take the elevated pathway, stay to the right when you come out of the turn. Hit the dash panels to remain at top speed. After a raised dash panel sends Sonic over a large divide, the elevated road will slope downward and meet the main road. Once it does, stick to the road's center to hit two dash panels.

Once you enter the narrow road between the cliffs and the sea, stick to the left side to hit a dash panel and collect a row of rings. Then, move to the road's right side to reach the next dash panel.

Item!

An item sits just past the entrance to the narrow cliffside walkway.

TIP

Use your Quick Step to quickly move from one side of the road to the other. It's good practice for the battle ahead.

A spring waits to welcome you back into town. Hit it and use Sonic's Homing Attack to take out two hovering robots and reach a rainbow ring. The rainbow ring shoots you to yet another high walkway, saving you precious seconds and allowing you to grab another item. More drifting, boosting, and dash paneling will see you to the main road's end.

Item!

This item is yours if you successfully execute the Homing Attacks required to reach the high walkway.

A bounce pad launches Sonic over a vast expanse and onto a long bridge. A large robot closes in, intent on ending the hedgehog's quest. There's nowhere for Sonic to hide, but there's plenty of room to run. The robot will slam the ground with

metallic arms; use Sonic's Quick Step to avoid them. If the robot's hands are together, Quick Step to the side of the road. the robot's hands are apart, stick to the center of the road. odge its arms until you hit a row of bounce pads.

After you land, the robot is now in front of you. Your objective is to repeatedly ram the robot using Sonic Boost. Remember that each Sonic Boost depletes a portion of your Boost Gauge, so pick up rings they pass by. Quick Step back and forth on the road to grab e rings, and then boost into the robot at every opportunity.

epeat the entire rocess until you destroy e metal behemoth; en get to the Goal ing as quickly as ossible. Deplete your oost Gauge completely, s time is of the essence.

GATHER RINGS AT TOP SPEED!

Type	Reward(s)	Items Found	Unlocks
Daytime	Moon Medal	—	—

Time	Reward
1'00'000	One Moon Medal, and tablet fragment adorned with a red jewel

ou must collect 100 rings before time runs out.

un forward and leap nto the second level. se a Homing Attack to each the spring, and it the dash panel as ou land. After the loop, it the spring and use wo Homing Attacks to each the rainbow ring. he ring will propel you to the distant rail.

Slide beneath two walls and speed to another bounce pad. Chain together three Homing Attacks and mount the second rail. Leap off the end of the rail to zip through two red rings and a rainbow ring.

Zip down the blue walkway to the bottom of the windmill. A raised dash panel launches Sonic into the air. Perform the correct button presses when prompted to reach the high walkway, which holds enough rings to clear the level.

NOTE

You have collected the first of two tablet fragments required to complete the first continent's Planet Tablet. The Planet Tablet is the key to the heart of the Gaia Temple.

Night falls on Apotos, and Sonic is transformed into Werehog form. But he isn't the only one affected by the sun's passing—some of the villagers have become uncharacteristically sad and gloomy.

Hey, don't cry!

VILLAGE: NIGHTTIME

Location	Name	Description	Unlocks	Rewards
Flower Street	Alexis	A young boy intrigued by the changes that occur to the town's residents at night	—	—
Cafe Terrace	Eric	Uninhabited until you speak to Gregorios	Sacred Shrine	First continent's Moon Tablet
Bell Square	Lambros	Lambros is taken aback by the nocturnal Sonic	—	Revisit to obtain Secret Soundtrack 33
Windmill Coast Street	Gregorios	The absentminded priest doesn't remember Sonic, but he mentions something about Eric and a yellow fox.	Cafe Terrace	—

Speak to Gregorios on Windmill Coast Street and he'll point you to Eric, who can be found at Cafe Terrace. Eric will give you the first continent's Moon Tablet. Head to the Sacred Shrine and use the Moon Tablet to open the door emblazoned with a crescent moon.

Item!

Revisit Lambros in Bell Square to obtain Secret Soundtrack 33.

Required Missions

DASH AND JUMP

Type	Reward(s)	Items Found	Unlocks
Nighttime	Sun Medal	—	Use those arms to get acrobatic!
Time	Reward		
1'00'000	One Sun Medal		

It's now time to get familiar with Sonic's Werehog form.

Move forward and jump over the spiked balls. In Werehog form, Sonic can perform a double-jump by tapping the Jump button a second time while in midair.

In Werehog form, Sonic can dash on all fours to gain speed and jump farther. Dash up to the cliff and jump over the ravine. Continue dashing until you reach the Goal Ring.

USE THOSE ARMS TO GET ACROBATIC!

Type	Reward(s)	Items Found	Unlocks
Nighttime	Sun Medal	—	Rack up an attack combo!
Time	Reward		
1'00'000	One Sun Medal		

You know what they say about a Werehog with big arms? A big reach. Time to use it!

Sonic can grab on to glowing ledges with his claws. Double-jump up the wall and use your arms to reach the ledge. Push up on the control stick to make Sonic hop onto the roof.

A pink targeting reticle means that Sonic is within range and is able to reach out and grab the glowing pole. Grab on to the pole and you'll start swinging back and forth. Push forward, release the pole, and jump safely over the spiked obstacles below.

Sonic can also grip and climb glowing poles. Latch on and push up on the control stick to begin climbing. Once you reach the top, tap the control stick left or right until Sonic's back is facing the way you ～sh to leap. Release the pole and jump while pushing the ～ntrol stick in the direction you wish to jump. In this case, push ～e control stick left, toward the Goal Ring.

Stand between the two boxes and pick up and throw each one at the approaching enemies. The boxes automatically respawn, so continue hurling them until the last enemy falls. The Goal Ring is offscreen, to the right.

NOTE — In order to deactivate a barrier and proceed, Sonic must defeat every enemy in the area.

RACK UP AN ATTACK COMBO!

Type	Reward(s)	Items Found	Unlocks
Nighttime	Sun Medal	—	Grab something, then throw!

Time	Reward
1'00'000	One Sun Medal

～'s time you learned how to claw your way through the competition.

～pproach an enemy ～d alternate swinging ～e Wii Remote and the ～unchuck to perform a ～mbo. You begin the ～me with a three-～ack combination (in ～erehog form, you ～ve two three-attack ～d two five-attack combinations) but will earn a five-attack ～mbo after you collect enough Dark Gaia Force. Finish off ～ery enemy to complete the mission.

NOTE — Single attacks are slow and weak. From here on out, always use combos or other special moves when attacking.

GRAB SOMETHING, THEN THROW!

Type	Reward(s)	Items Found	Unlocks
Nighttime	Sun Medal	—	Let fly the Were-Hammer!

Time	Reward
1'00'000	One Sun Medal

～here's a time to be sharp and a time to be blunt. In this mission, forego your ～aws for wooden crates.

LET FLY THE WERE-HAMMER!

Type	Reward(s)	Items Found	Unlocks
Nighttime	Sun Medal	—	—

Time	Reward
1'00'000	One Sun Medal

Insert your favorite hammer pun here.

The Were-Hammer isn't terribly powerful, but it does drive the baddies back a bit. It's also very useful for knocking flying foes out of the air. Drop the hammer on a few enemies and the mission is complete.

ACT 1: MOONLIT TOWN

Type	Reward(s)	Items Found	Unlocks
Nighttime	Sun Medal	Secret Movie 2, Secret Illustration 23, Secret Illustration 59	Act II: Moonsoaked Alleys

Ranking	Reward
S	Three Sun Medals
A	Two Sun Medals
B	One Sun Medal

Target time for this mission is seven minutes.

Item!

When the mission begins, turn around and follow the path to retrieve a cleverly hidden item.

When a barrier appears, you must defeat every enemy within its boundaries before proceeding. Three-hit combos are sufficient to lay these creatures to rest.

NOTE

Grab rings to replenish Sonic's health. Defeat enemies, destroy objects, and find Force containers to gain Dark Gaia Force and fill the Unleash Gauge.

Climb up the pole and leap to the nearby ledge. Approach and raise the door and move along the path. Three enemies confront you; smash them using successive combo attacks.

Continue along the path until a cutscene reveals a barrier with a strange symbol. You must collect three Dark Energy Keys in order to deactivate the force field. The first one is directly ahead, sitting in the middle of the road.

The second Dark Energy Key rests on a blue awning at the far end of an outdoor cafe. You must defeat all the enemies before you can continue.

Item!

An item is hidden behind the brown crates at the rear corner of the outdoor cafe.

The third Dark Energy Key is far away. Continue through the city, defeating any challengers until you reach the glowing horizontal pole. Jump up, grab hold of it, and then leap to the glowing ledge on the far wall. Haul yourself up and continue on.

Item!

An item sits below the bell in a small alcove on the rooftops Climb up the vertical glowing pole next to the two-story building. Leap onto the nearby rooftop and across the gaps to the third building. Grab the item and hop back down to the street.

Lift the door near the barrier to reveal the third and final Dark Energy Key. Once you have it, the barrier automatically drops.

Your victory is short-lived, as more dark meanies rush to greet you. The first wave attacks in a tight group, so one or two combinations should finish them all off. The second wave of enemies is more elusive, so chase them down one at a time and give them a little personal attention.

Enter the small dwelling and climb the vertical pole to reach the Goal Ring.

ACT II: MOONSOAKED ALLEYS

Type	Reward(s)	Items Found	Unlocks
Nighttime	Sun Medal	Secret Illustration 30, Secret Illustration 64, Secret Illustration 66, Secret Movie 3	Act III: Hill Beneath Starry Skies

Ranking	Reward
S	Three Sun Medals
A	Two Sun Medals
B	One Sun Medal

arget time for this mission is seven minutes.

Destroy the planters to reveal a button. Stand on the button to open the door.

now you know the ill—defeat all enemies drop the barrier. To ake better time, dash own the road, crashing to breakables and llecting rings along e way.

Item!

An item sits in a small house off the road's left-hand side, just before the road bends to the left.

These Killer Bees are real pests. Use your Were-Hammer to knock them down, and then finish them off with a three-hit combination. If you're having trouble connecting, hurl a crate at them instead.

Dash toward the break in the road and leap over the chasm. Enter the tunnel and engage the Nightmares and Killer Bees before proceeding.

Item!

This item can be reached by standing on the platform below the first glowing block and dash jumping straight out, away from the building with a double-jump timed before you start falling. You will land on a roof with an item on it.

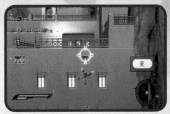 

After exiting the tunnel, take the stairs all the way up and leap to the far landing. Reach out and grab the lowest glowing block. Pull yourself up and move the control stick up to target the next ledge. Spin and release your grip to hop upward. Grab on to the next block and move the control stick left in order to aim for the adjacent block. Release your grip and grab on to the left-hand ledge. Finally, aim for the roof and release your grip.

Grab the glowing ledge and move the control stick left to make Sonic shimmy around the corner. Once the landing is below your feet, release your grip on the ledge.

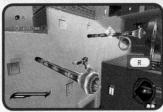 

The next acrobatic feat requires you to leap from one horizontal bar to another. Grab on to the first one and you'll automatically begin swinging back and forth. As you swing toward the next bar, release your grip. Sonic's momentum will carry him toward it. Simply reach out and grab it once it is targeted. To leap to the landing, release your grip when you are moving toward it. If you come up short, tap the Jump button to give you a little extra distance.

Item!

An item is on the rooftops above the poles you just navigated. Run up the first flight of stairs and hop onto the roof to get it.

The next obstacle requires you to leap from one vertical glowing pole to another. Grab on to the first one and head to its top. Move the control stick left or right until Sonic's back is facing the other pole. Release your grip, leap from the pole, and quickly grab on to the next one. Repeat the process to make the final jump onto the path and be on your way.

Flip this switch to activate the lift. Move onto the platform to ride the elevator down. A horde of Nightmares and Killer Bees are anxious to make your acquaintance. Greet them with combination attacks and Were-Hammers. Use the crates to destroy multiple Killer Bees with each throw.

If your life is low, refill it by collecting the rings around the perimeter of the overlook.

Once the battle is over, slide down the glowing pole by grabbing on to it and then releasing your grip. Do the same with the second glowing pole to reach ground level.

Item!

After sliding down the first pole, hop left to the pillar's top and then creep over a horizontal ledge. Raise the stone door and the item is yours.

A lengthy ledge-crawl is the next order of business. Creep over the lower ledge until you are directly beneath the upper ledge. Grab on to the upper ledge and shimmy across to a rocky outcropping. Tread carefully upon a third ledge to reach the walkway that leads to the Goal Ring.

ACT III: HILL BENEATH STARRY SKIES

Type	Reward(s)	Items Found	Unlocks
Nighttime	Sun Medal	Secret Illustration 26, Secret Illustration 65, Secret Illustration 67, tablet fragment adorned with a blue jewel	Spagoni

Ranking	Reward
S	Three Sun Medals
A	Two Sun Medals
B	One Sun Medal

Target time for this mission is seven minutes.

Item!

An item is hidden behind a broken wall, just to the left of three large dog statues.

The multitude of Nightmares that appear after you climb the first flight of stairs are no match for your newly acquired five-hit combination attack.

The second Dark Energy Key is in a broken structure to the right of the main path. After you grab it, a group of Nightmares ambushes you. Finish them off and continue your nighttime hike.

NOTE
If you haven't earned enough Force to unlock the longer combination, make sure you do so on this level. The missions get harder from here on out, and the five-hit combination is essential for success.

Use your combination attack to shatter this rock wall. Be on the lookout for additional breakable walls scattered throughout the stage, as they generally conceal an important object.

The third and final ring is just beyond a breakable wall. Perform a little smash-and-grab to bring down the barrier.

You know the drill: It takes three Dark Energy Keys to disable the barrier. The first is in plain sight, just inside the door of this ruined structure.

Just past the barrier is a courtyard with a fountain at its center. Approach it and a large force of Gaia grunts attack. Execute your combos, use the boxes as weapons, and refill your health with the nearby rings. Once the battle is over, head up the path to the Goal Ring.

Before you reach the second Dark Energy Key, you must exterminate the swarm of Killer Bees. Use the crates scattered around the room to make quick work of the busy bees.

With both halves of the first tablet in hand, it's off to Spagonia University to seek out Professor Pickle, an expert on Dark Gaia lore. Perhaps he can shed some light on the darkness overtaking the planet.

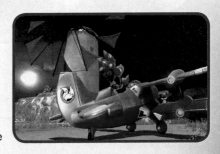

Spagonia

Spagonia is a bustling and heavily populated city that includes a university.

VILLAGE: DAYTIME

Location	Name	Description	Unlocks	Rewards
Main Street	Lucia and Ippolita	A cute but unhelpful pair of kids	—	—
Baker Street	Denise	She's heard of the professor, but that's all	—	—
Back Alley	Assistant	Ask "Where is the laboratory?" for directions	Pickle Lab	—
Pickle Lab	Professor Pickle	The professor has been kidnapped by Eggman	Mazuri	—

Sonic and Chip arrive in Spagonia, only to find out that Professor Pickle has been kidnapped by Eggman! After searching Pickle's Laboratory, Tails, whom you met in the cutscene, concludes that a mysterious hole in Mazuri might provide a clue to the professor's whereabouts.

Mazuri

Mazuri is a small tribal village of hunter-gatherers.

VILLAGE: NIGHTTIME

Location	Name	Description	Unlocks	Rewards
The Holy Tree	N/A	Uninhabited during the night	—	—
The Hunter's Home	N/A	Uninhabited during the night	—	Revisit after defeating the Egg Beetle for Secret Soundtrack 35
Shop	N/A	Uninhabited during the night	—	—
Lookout Tower	N/A	Uninhabited during the night	Mysterious Hole	—
Mysterious Hole	Professor Pickle	Professor Pickle is held captive here	—	—

Sonic, Chip, and Tails arrive to a deserted village, but they glimpse a mysterious hole after visiting each location. Upon investigating, they find a famished professor locked in Eggman's cell. Once freed and safely returned to his Spagonia laboratory, he tells the story of Dark Gaia's premature awakening and the possibility of fixing the planet by restoring the Chaos Emeralds. Sonic must visit Gaia Temples and utilize their power to restore the Chaos Emeralds. The Chaos Emeralds will, in turn, heal the planet. Next stop, Mazuri Village.

VILLAGE: DAYTIME

Location	Name	Description	Unlocks	Rewards
...e Holy Tree	Gwek	The thankful village elder	Sacred Shrine	First continent's Planet Tablet
...e Hunter's Home	Kwami	A vigilant villager	—	Secret Soundtrack 35 (visit at night, after defeating Egg Beetle)
...op	Ana	Answer, "Nah, it's a lot of fun!"	—	Secret Soundtrack 34
...okout Tower	Kofi	Villager with knowledge of ancient drawings	—	—
...cred Shrine	N/A	The first continent's Gaia Gate	—	—

...ek the Elder is a
...ple Guardian and
...the knowledge to
...air the two halves of
...table fragment. The
...ult is the first conti-
...t's Planet Tablet, a
...that will allow you
...nter the Gaia Gate
...in the Sacred Shrine.

Item!

...peak to Ana at the shop and tell her that traveling
...e world is a lot of fun. She'll admire your attitude
...d give you Secret Soundtrack 34.

...e the Planet Tablet on
...door emblazoned
...a glowing star.

Required Missions

BOSS: EGG BEETLE

Type	Reward(s)	Items Found	Unlocks
...aytime	Moon Medal	—	—

Time	Ranking	Reward
20'000	S	One Moon Medal!

...man and Sonic meet on the road to the Gaia Temple. The reunion is not friendly.

NOTE

Any time greater than 2'20
yields a "C" ranking and no Moon Medal is
awarded.

The treetop road is
wide enough for Sonic
to take evasive action
in response to the Egg
Beetle's various attacks.
Use Quick Step to avoid
the metallic crates that
the beetle drops on the
path. Give them a wide
berth, as they periodically change positions.

TIP

Be sure to collect rings to fill up your
Boost Gauge.

When the Egg Beetle
spreads its claws, use
Sonic Boost to ram the
metal monstrosity and
inflict damage. Do this
even if the claws are
ignited, but be quick
or the powerful pincers
will take their toll on our
intrepid hero.

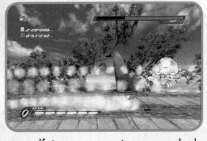

After you've inflicted
enough damage, the
perspective changes
to side-scroller. The
Egg Beetle fires three
missiles that approach
from Sonic's rear. Move
toward the front (right)
of the screen to give
yourself time to react. Jump over the lowest missile and remain
on the road to allow the two higher projectiles room to pass
overhead.

After firing the missiles, the Egg Beetle takes position to Sonic's side and attempts to use its pincers. To avoid the pincers, jump above them just as they begin closing. When the Egg Beetle moves in front of Sonic, use a Homing Attack to inflict more damage. Repeat the process until you defeat the Egg Beetle.

After squashing the Egg Beetle, Sonic and Chip visit the Gaia Temple and renew the first Chaos Emerald. As foretold in the Gaia manuscripts, the power of the Chaos Emerald repairs the first continent. The next step is to visit the professor Spagonia for clues to the next temple's location.

NOTE

When a continent is restored, you can visit any village on that continent and manually switch between night and day.

Item!

Before heading to Spagonia, revisit Mazuri and switch to nighttime. Speak to Kwami in the Hunter's Home. Tell him you know that you are in Mazuri, and he'll reward you with Secret Soundtrack 35!

SONIC UNLEASHED™

RESTORING THE SECOND CONTINENT

Spagonia

VILLAGE: NIGHTTIME

Location	Name	Description	Unlocks	Rewards
Main Street	Lucia and Ippolita	Uninhabited until after visiting Professor Pickle	—	Second continent's Moon Tablet
Baker Street	Denise	A protective mother figure	—	Secret Soundtrack 39 (after visiting Prof. Pickle)
Back Alley	Assistant	The moon has an adverse effect on the assistant	Pickle Lab	—
Aqueduct Street	Otto	An absentminded old man	—	—
Pickle Lab	Professor Pickle	A brilliant, thin man with a large appetite	Sacred Shrine, Holoska	—

Professor Pickle has deciphered more of the Gaia Manuscript and has located one Sacred Shrine right here in Spagonia and one on the far continent of Holoska. After you leave his laboratory, revisit Lucia and Ippolita on Main Street. They'll provide you with the second continent's Moon Tablet, which will unlock the Moon Door in Spagonia's Sacred Shrine and allow you to play the continent's nighttime missions.

Five-hit combos are the answers to any Nightmare problem.

Item!

Visit Denise on Baker Street after meeting with Professor Pickle. She'll give you Secret Soundtrack 39.

Item!

An item is hidden behind three breakable urns, just past the first barrier.

Required Missions

ACT I: ALLEYS OF SPAGONIA

Type	Reward(s)	Items Found	Unlocks
Nighttime	—	Secret Document 1, Secret Movie 4, Secret Movie 9, Secret Illustration 15, Secret Illustration 24, Secret Illustration 77, Secret Illustration 79	Act II: Jet Black Back Streets

Ranking	Reward
S	Three Sun Medals
A	Two Sun Medals
B	One Sun Medal

Target time for this mission is eight minutes.

Item!

After you raise the stone door, look behind the fruit stand for another hidden item.

Flying bad guys require different tactics to defeat. Use your Were-Hammer or knock them down while attacking in midair. Follow a midair assault with a combination attack to finish them off.

The metal door is too heavy to raise, even for Sonic. Grab the nearby metal crate and place it on the blue switch to gain entry.

When you enter the cathedral courtyard, many enemies rush to attack you. On the bigger foes, open with a Were-Wallop and then finish the job with a combination attack.

NOTE

Attack combinations inflict greater damage to enemies that were previously damaged by a Were-Wallop.

A barrier rises at the cathedral's base. Sonic must find three Dark Energy Keys to disable it. The first is on top of the fountain. Leap from the walkway banister in front of the cathedral to get it.

To obtain the second and third Dark Energy Keys, you must scale the cathedral. Use Sonic's long reach to climb to the church's second story, then run around to the left to find the second ring.

The third ring is in the clock tower. Climb to the third floor, hop onto the planter between the two towers, and double-jump upward, using Sonic's arms to grab the high, glowing ledge.

Item!

While you're enjoying the view from the clock tower, double-jump to the other tower to grab an item.

With the barrier disabled, continue through the city. Killer Bees infest a small courtyard, so use the wooden crates to end their incessant buzzing.

Pull the lever to activate the lift and then hop onto the moving platform to reach the second floor.

Item!

On the second floor, move up the first flight of stairs and hop onto the ledge between the gap in the wrought-iron fence. From there, leap onto the structure on the alley's far side to get the item.

To traverse the two uneven horizontal bars, Sonic must perform some relatively easy acrobatics. By now, swinging from bar to bar should be fairly effortless.

reach the distant
oal Ring, you can
ch a ride from the
nhostile Dark Bats, or
u can use the narrow
dge on the roof's
ght side to reach the
cond building.

Item!

Leap from the first building to the alleyway below to find this item.

n the second building,
stroy the baddie with
well-thrown crate or
midair attack; then
pproach the edge
the building. The
arby Dark Bat will be
rgeted automatically.
rab hold and enjoy
e ride.

On the third building, use midair attacks to take out the pests on the rooftop. The fourth building is reachable by a simple jump.

Item!

Fall off the left side of the fourth building to reach this item. Use a glowing, vertical pole to climb back up to the rooftop.

A jump is all it takes to reach the Goal Ring from the final rooftop. However, make sure you grab the item that sits behind it before you touch the ring.

Item!

Avoid touching the Goal Ring; instead, move around it to the rear of the rooftop. Descend a short ramp and then leap onto the structure upon which the item sits. After grabbing the item, a glowing pole will allow you to return to the Goal Ring.

ACT II: JET BLACK BACK STREETS

Type	Reward(s)	Items Found	Unlocks
Nighttime	—	Secret Movie 5, Secret Illustration 38, Illustration 70	Act III: The Great Aqueduct
Ranking		Reward	
S		Three Sun Medals	
A		Two Sun Medals	
B		One Sun Medal	

Target time for this mission is six minutes.

Spikes are a new hazard for the Werehog. Jump over them or wait until they recede to safely run over them.

> **TIP**
> Taking out flying bad guys is easier if you start your attack on or near the shadow they cast.

TIP

When jumping, pay attention to Sonic's shadow to gauge distance. If it looks like he isn't going to make it, tap Jump while in midair to perform a double-jump.

The enemies that appear within the long covered walkway will slow Sonic down. Use combos to dispel the Nightmares, and use the wooden crates to crush the Killer Bees. You can pick up the Frights and hurl them at one another to make them easier to target with combos.

Item!

Instead of following the main path to the right, grab onto the first glowing block stuck to the alley wall and fling yourself upward. Grab on to the second one and use it to reach the high ledge and the item upon it.

Item!

The alley forks here. Take the right path to reach a distant item. If you're going for speed, ignore this path and head straight at the fork.

Step on this green button to lower the spikes and activate the buzz saws ahead. Hop over the saws or time your passing to escape unscathed.

A new baddie appears to make your acquaintance: the Power Master. Open with a Were-Wallop and finish with a combo attack; then turn your attention to its cohorts.

Item!

In the area after the covered walkway, be sure to leave a crate intact. After defeating all the enemies use the crate to access the small bridge above this area.

Stepping on the green button will activate the alley's defenses, including spikes and buzz saws, but it will also activate a lift near where you encountered the Master. Backtrack, avoiding the hazards, and leap onto the moving platform.

Leap from platform to pole and from pole to platform, using the Werehog's long reach. Remember to double-jump while in the air if necessary to reach the next pole or platform—you must do this on the last leap to the green button.

Step onto the green button to make the ga below rise. Hop down and proceed through the opening to the Go Ring.

ACT III: THE GREAT AQUEDUCT

Type	Reward(s)	Items Found	Unlock
Nighttime	—	Secret Movie 12, Secret Illustration 20, Secret Document 2, tablet fragment adorned with a blue jewel	—

Ranking	Reward
S	Three Sun Medals
A	Two Sun Medals
B	One Sun Medal

Target time for this mission is nine minutes.

Item!

To reach this item, move past the glowing pole and destroy the urns in the alcove on the walkway's left side.

You can either hang and shimmy across this glowing ledge or simply sidestep on top of it.

Climb the glowing pole and hop onto the aqueduct's second story. A barrier rises, requiring you to seek out three Dark Energy Keys. Move along the walkway and hitch a ride on the Dark Bat. Defeat the Frights on the other side and hitch a second ride over the next broken section.

Climb the vertical glowing pole to the aqueduct's top. Backtrack down the narrow walkway until you reach a lift. Hop on and take the elevator down to the second Dark Energy Key. Ride the lift back to the aqueduct's top. If you're collecting items, continue backtracking until you are directly above your starting point. If you are racing against the clock, ignore the item and head back to the orange pole.

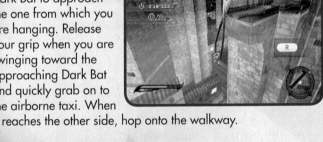

Wait for the second Dark Bat to approach the one from which you are hanging. Release your grip when you are swinging toward the approaching Dark Bat and quickly grab on to the airborne taxi. When it reaches the other side, hop onto the walkway.

Once your feet are planted firmly on the ground, turn around and head to Sonic's right, backtracking to the walkway's far edge. Hitch a ride on a Dark Bat to reach the first Dark Energy Key.

Item!

Once you're on top of the aqueduct, backtrack until you are just over your starting position. A lift on the walkway's far side will take you down to the item.

Move to the far end of the second-story walkway and slide down a horizontal pole to ground level. Defeat the Frights to claim the third Dark Energy Key.

CAUTION

Navigating the narrow walkway is precarious at best. Hug the fence when available and proceed carefully when there is no fence.

Whether or not you grab the item, it's now time to return to the aqueduct's second story. Slide down the same pole you used to reach the upper walkway.

Return to the upper walkway by climbing up both glowing vertical poles. Take a right and head toward the distant Goal Ring. Drop down from your high perch and approach the goal. A Fright Master and his cronies rise up to attack. Concentrate your assaults on the Master so it doesn't have time to summon any more enemies. Either throw the Frights at it or rush and stun it with sonic's Were-Claw attack.

Item!

A well-hidden item is concealed by three jars and a large support structure at the far end of the second-story walkway. You can't see it, so destroy the jars to nab it.

TIP

If you aren't concerned with time, let the Master summon more and more enemies so you can rack up the Dark Gaia Force.

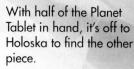

With half of the Planet Tablet in hand, it's off to Holoska to find the other piece.

Holoska

Holoska is a cold, snow-covered, one-family village.

VILLAGE: DAYTIME

Location	Name	Description	Unlocks	Rewards
Central Bonfire	Jari-Pekka	A strange fellow who might not be as odd as he appears	—	—
Food Storage Area	Sarianna	A worried wife	Storage Area, Family Home	—
Storage Area	Jari-Thure	Sarianna's cowering husband	—	—
Family Home	Marketa	The protective daughter	Food Storage Area (new dialogue)	Revisit for Secret Soundtrack 36
Food Storage Area (revisited)	Sarianna	A worried wife	Sacred Shrine	Fourth continent's Sun Tablet
Sacred Shrine	Fourth Temple	The fourth continent's Gaia Gate	—	—

Getting in the middle of a family squabble leads you to Holoska's Sacred Shrine. Tell Sarianna you'll check out the shrine in her husband's place, and she'll mark the location on your map. She'll also give you the fourth continent's Sun Tablet, which will allow you to open the Sacred Shrine's Sun Door.

Item!

After Sarianna marks the location of the Sacred Shrine on your map, visit Marketa in the family home to receive Secret Soundtrack 36.

Required Missions

DIVE-BOMB THE ENEMY WITH A STOMP!

Type	Reward(s)	Items Found	Unlocks
Daytime	Moon Medal	—	Head for the goal!

Use Sonic's Stomp to damage enemies and destroy obstacles.

Jump above the ice and perform a Stomp to break through.

HEAD FOR THE GOAL RING

Type	Reward(s)	Items Found	Unlocks
Daytime	Moon Medal	Secret Illustration 33, Secret Illustration 73, Secret Document 9	Gather rings at top speed

Time	Ranking	Reward
3'20'000	S	Three Moon Medals
1'20'000	A	Two Moon Medals
2'00'000	B	One Moon Medal

Utilize all that you've learned to reach the Goal Ring as quickly as possible.

Sonic gets to rest his feet for a spell while he lets the toboggan do the work. As you speed down the half-pipe, stick to the outside of the turns to hit the dash panels. Once you jump onto open ice, the dash panels are generally centered on the path.

NOTE

You can drift in the toboggan, but you can't perform Sonic's Quick Step.

Ice chunks fall onto the path and will stop the toboggan dead in its tracks. Stay in the middle to avoid them and hit the dash panels.

Navigate the switchbacks by moving the control stick in the appropriate direction. You can also jump the toboggan to reach the floating ring. Once the switchbacks are behind you, be prepared to pull off a series of four jumps over spike hazards. One final jump and you'll leave the sled behind.

Sonic lands on a rail for a short grind session. Jump before the rail ends to reach the next piece of rail. This is faster than taking the lower path.

Item!

If you wish to sacrifice a little time for an item, put on the brakes as you travel over the descending ice blocks. You'll fall down to a couple of rails that lead to an item.

You must use Sonic's Stomp to break through the ice here. After you do, quickly jump from the unstable platform in order to take the faster high road.

Once you enter the large ice cavern, boost over the Egg Shackles or fall victim to their explosions.

TIP

Boost to shake off an Egg Shackle that has attached itself to Sonic.

Item!

An item sits on the main path just past the Egg Shackles. Grab it as you navigate through the falling ice chunks.

Jump as you approach these small concrete structures, then use a Homing Attack on the robots that guard them. Finally, Stomp through the ice clogging their center. Running full speed into their sides will knock you back, costing valuable seconds.

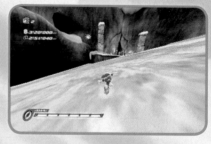

Boost over this tilting ice sheet. Homing Attacks work as well, but if you time it wrong you'll be electrocuted and stunned for a few seconds.

This long corridor is perfect for a couple of successive boosts. Once you near the exit, be prepared to jump onto an elevated rail. This allows you to bypass a more circuitous and time-consuming route.

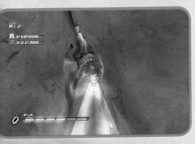

Perform a few Homing Attacks here to reach the high rail.

Item!

If you make the rail, an item is yours without any additional effort or fancy maneuvering.

Stomp through the ice here to shave off precious seconds from your final tally.

Once you break through the ice crystals, you're home free. Empty your Boost Gauge and hit the Goal Ring at top speed.

GATHER RINGS AT TOP SPEED!

Type	Reward(s)	Items Found	Unlocks
Daytime	Moon Medal	—	Don't break anything along the way!
Collect 150 rings in 1'45.			

Jump the toboggan to pick up an easy five rings.

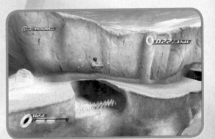

Successfully complete this series of jumps to grab about 30 more rings.

Chain two Homing Attacks together to reach the upper rail that holds many rings.

Fall through this ice bridge to rack up more rings.

Hop off this unstable ice section and use a Lightspeed Dash to gather the rings that float just overhead. A little farther and you'll have all 150 rings.

DON'T BREAK ANYTHING ALONG THE WAY!

Type	Reward(s)	Items Found	Unlocks
Daytime	Moon Medal, tablet fragment adorned with a red jewel	—	Time attack! Race for the goal!

You break it, you buy it.

Follow the onscreen button presses to defeat each of the three Nightmares and save the villagers.

Resist the urge to reach top speed until after you navigate the first couple ice obstacles; use Quick Step if necessary.

Upon further analysis of the Gaia Manuscripts, the professor has gleaned the location of another Gaia Temple. Head to Chun-nan and talk to the villagers to learn more.

NOTE

The key to success on this stage is to be quick but not in a hurry. Slow down if you're about to run into an ice crystal; you have enough time to be careful.

Use Homing Attacks to easily navigate the maze of ice. Fortunately, "don't break anything" doesn't refer to enemies.

Hit the dash panels in the final corridor to ensure you avoid the last several crystals.

With the tablet's second half in hand, it's time to visit the professor. Hopefully he'll have figured out the next step. When you return to Spagonia, you discover something is amiss. The Dark Gaia's power has influenced the villagers.

Chun-nan

The village elder is missing. Speak to the villagers to see if you can help find him.

VILLAGE: NIGHTTIME

Location	Name	Description	Unlocks	Rewards
Restaurant	Chun	A young boy with a healthy appetite	—	—
Lantern Herbal Shop	Lin	An elderly woman who enlists your help	Waterflow Way (new dialogue)	—
Waterflow Way	Shuifon	A man with an important item	Sacred Shrine	Third continent's Moon Tablet
Street Bench	Hualin	A young, curious woman	—	Secret Soundtrack 41
The Back Gate	N/A	Uninhabited at night	—	—
Sacred Shrine	Third Temple	The third Gaia Gate	—	—

If you decide to help Lin and the village elder, he'll direct you to Shuifon at Waterflow Way. He'll give you the third continent's Moon Tablet, which will allow you to enter the Sacred Shrine's Moon Door.

ACT I: THE SACRED SHRINE

Type	Reward(s)	Items Found	Unlocks
Nighttime	—	Secret Movie 13, Secret Illustration 84, Illustration 81	Act II: Rising Dragon Falls
Ranking		Reward	
S		Three Sun Medals	
A		Two Sun Medals	
B		One Sun Medal	

Target time for this mission is nine minutes.

Required Missions

Breakable doors and walls are scattered throughout the level. Use a combo to quickly destroy them and gain entry.

Item!

An item sits behind the breakable door against the right side of the long, gently curving corridor.

This area requires some precision jumping over deep water. Look for your shadow; it'll show you where you're going to land.

Item!

In this next area, a hidden path under the bridge leads to another item. Traverse the swings and jumps to a small island, then ride to safety on the Dark Bat.

Wait for the glowing pole to move toward you, then grab it. Climb to the top, and when the second pole gets close, jump over to it. Remember, Sonic's back should face the direction you wish to jump.

Don't waste time worrying about which of the bridge's walkways, upper or lower, you should be on. They both lead to the same place. Use the Dark Bat to cross the small gap between the bridge and the walkway.

Scale this glowing pole to reach the structure's roof.

Item!

Take the path to the right of the green pole to obtain an item.

There are two ways to go once you reach the roof. Take the right path first and enter a large room. Defeat the bad guys and pull the lever to deactivate the force field. Backtrack and take the left path up two flights of stairs. Jump from one glowing horizontal pole to the next in order to reach the Goal Ring.

ACT II: RISING DRAGON FALLS

Type	Reward(s)	Items Found	Unlocks
Nighttime	—	Secret Illustration 27, Secret Illustration 68, Secret Illustration 78, Secret Movie 6	Act III: Path to Darkness

Ranking	Reward
S	Three Sun Medals
A	Two Sun Medals
B	One Sun Medal

Target time for this mission is nine minutes

A tough battle ensues in the multilevel area. Remember to target the Power Masters first because they do the most damage.

Item!

After your first enemy encounter, the path curves to the left into a narrow bridge. T find an item, destroy the urns that sit to the bridge's right.

Time your passage to avoid the swinging blades. Dash if you need more speed.

The ground here is unstable; it collapses as you approach, revealing spike hazards. Dash and jump, and then double-jump while in the air to make it safely across.

Item!

Just past the unstable ground and the pair of bladed pendulums is an item. Look behind the boxes on the path's right to find it.

Clear this ravine by dashing and jumping.

Item!

After you clear the ravine, move right to what appears to be a dead end. Wait for the Dark Bat to approach and hitch a ride. Follow the path to reach the item and then backtrack to the main path.

44

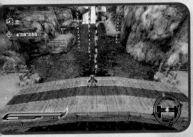

It gets difficult from here on out. The area ahead contains three moving glowing poles. Leap out and grab the first one, then climb to the top. When the second pole gets close, jump to it. Wait for it to pass near the third pole and make the grab. Once you reach the third pole, leap from it to the rocky outcropping on your left.

om the outcropping, grab on to a Dark Bat that'll put you in aping distance of a fourth, stationary pole. Jump and latch on it. Climb to its apex and leap to the horizontal pole planted in e cliff wall. From there it's just a short hop to solid ground.

Item!

The main path leads up, toward the waterfall. However, a narrow path leads down, toward the base of the waterfall. Follow the narrow path down and behind the falls to find an item stashed in a small alcove.

's time to scale the ace of the waterfall. he bad news is there re no guardrails or afety nets. Take your me navigating these azards and you'll do ust fine. First, jump over ne first chasm and grab n to the narrow ledge. Pull yourself up and continue on.

Make a second leaping grab to another ledge and proceed up the path to a vertical pole.

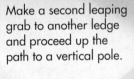

Double-jump from the first pole onto the outcropping to your left. Wait for the Dark Bat to approach, and jump straight up to grab hold. Ride across the divide and either leap directly onto the vertical pole or to the large outcropping. Climb to the pole's top and position Sonic so his back is facing the nearby horizontal pole.

Leap to one horizontal pole and then to another. The final jump to the vertical pole is a long one, so make sure you are swinging toward it before you release your grip. Double-jump in midair and then reach out and grab the pole. Climb up it, collecting the rings as you ascend.

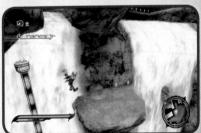

From the pole's top, leap to the Dark Bat and hitch a ride over the vast expanse. jump over to a hanging pole and then onto a low platform. Hug the wall as you pass behind the waterfall and climb the last vertical pole.

Hop to the rocks above the waterfall, and the worst is now behind you!

Dash through the first leg of the mission breaking jars and picking up rings along the way. Leap over the chasm and run up to the first structure.

Be careful when traversing this narrow log. One misstep and you'll be washed over the falls. When you reach the other side, walk toward the screen's bottom and make one last leap across the water.

If you're racing the clock, climb up and over the first structure to avoid a lengthy battle inside.

Douse the fire by throwing a barrel of water at it. If you miss, don't worry; water barrels automatically reappear after each use.

 **Item!**

An item sits on the roof of the first structure.

Use the glowing block and ledge to scale the wall. Once on top, several enemies desperately try to keep you from reaching the nearby Goal Ring. Obviously, they underestimate your tenacity.

Approach the switch. Rotate the control stick to lower the bridge. However, don't lower it all of the way, because an item sits underneath.

Show them who's in charge and then race for the goal.

ACT III: PATH TO DARKNESS

Type	Reward(s)	Items Found	Unlocks
Nighttime	—	Secret Movie 7, Secret Illustration 53, Secret Illustration 82, Secret Soundtrack 19, tablet fragment adorned with a blue jewel	Boss—Dark Gaia Phoenix

Ranking	Reward
S	Three Sun Medals
A	Two Sun Medals
B	One Sun Medal
Target time for this mission is nine minutes.	

Lower the bridge just enough to leave a gap between it and the far side. Drop through the gap and take the item.

These Egg Typhoons will blow you backward and possibly off the broken walkway. Use boxes to destroy them from a distance, or wait until they start blowing and then jump next to them to attack up close.

Cross a ravine by grabbing and swinging from two horizontal poles; then carefully leap from one outcropping to the next until you reach the upper walkway. Travel down the walkway and use a glowing ledge to climb up to a rocky platform.

cross above this oken section of alkway, hop and ab on to three Dark ats. Wait for the third ark Bat to move within nge before leaping it.

Destroy the Dark Gaia Forces and continue your trek to the top of the mountain.

Item!

A section of walkway gives way beneath Sonic's feet just before you reach this item. Dash and double-jump to cross the divide and reach the item.

This area takes some skilled jumping to clear. To start, hop over the three floating platforms.

Douse the flames with the water-filled barrel and then continue on.

Item!

Walk off the first floating platform to reach the item sitting on a stone pillar below. A Dark Bat appears to facilitate your return to the upper platforms.

After you successfully traverse the first three platforms, the path splits. Take the right path only if you wish to collect a Force container. Otherwise, move left, leaping from one rock pillar to the next until you reach the large central platform.

When you reach the central platform, a new enemy appears—the Cyclops. This is a giant, lumbering hulk that carries a very big club. Fortunately, it moves slowly. Attack quickly, ready to leap over or away from its club attacks. If you take damage, hop to the surrounding platforms and pick up the rings and replenish your health.

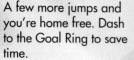

Follow the Dark Gaia Phoenix and climb onto the nearest raised platform. Grab the water-filled barrel and throw it at the Phoenix to douse the flame barrier that surrounds it. Then, follow it to the central platform and wait for it to land. When it touches down, hit it with all you've got. Combinations work well and do a lot of damage.

A few more jumps and you're home free. Dash to the Goal Ring to save time.

BOSS: DARK GAIA PHOENIX

Type	Reward(s)	Items Found	Unlocks
Nighttime	Sun Medal	—	Spagonia Day, Chun-nan Day
Time			Reward
1'00'000			One Sun Medal
Any time greater than 5'00 yields a "C" ranking and no Sun Medal is awarded.			

After damaging the feathered foe, follow the onscreen button presses to inflict even more damage.

The village elder lies unconscious in the courtyard, and the benevolent Gaia Temple guardian has been corrupted by Dark Gaia. Defeat the Phoenix to return it to its natural state and to save the elder.

Return to the raised platform once again to soak the flaming feather-head. You'll need to connect with two barrels to remove the shield the second time and three barrels the third time. Be quick when going for the barrels, as the bird will fire sharp quills at Sonic. keep moving to successfully dodge them.

Repeat the process until Dark Gaia's influence on the magnificent bird is broken.

You've succeeded in rescuing the village elder, Zonshen. As a reward, he offers to combine the tablet fragments and form the third continent's Planet Tablet.

The Gaia Temple responds to the intact tablet and refills another Chaos Emerald. Renewed, the Choas Emerald restores the third continent. The Phoenix rises from the ashes, free from the Curse of Dark Gaia and able to return to its rightful place as the temple guardian.

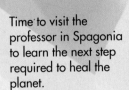

Meanwhile, Eggman enjoys a sandwich while he receives a status report on the slow progress of his Dark Gaia–powered Land Construction System. It appears he awakened Dark Gaia too early, and the malevolent force couldn't sustain its own weight. As a result, it became dispersed, not powerful enough to fulfill Eggman's evil plans.

Time to visit the professor in Spagonia to learn the next step required to heal the planet.

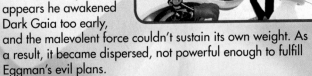

RESTORING THE THIRD CONTINENT
Spagonia

Visit Otto on Aqueduct Street to obtain the second continent's Sun Tablet. The Sacred Shrine now appears on the village map. Enter it and use the Sun Tablet on the Sun Door.

Hit the raised dash panel at the hill's top to make it through the rainbow ring and give yourself an extra boos

Item!
At the U-turn, smash the three boxes on the right. Under them you'll find an item and a dash panel.

HEAD FOR THE GOAL RING!

Type	Reward(s)	Items Found	Unlocks
Daytime	Moon Medal(s), Secret Hint 7	Secret Document 6, Secret Document 7, Illustration 9, Illustration 37	Gather rings at top speed.

Time	Ranking	Reward
2'50'000	S	Three Moon Medals
1'20'000	A	Two Moon Medals
2'00'000	B	One Moon Medal

Utilize all that you've learned to reach the Goal Ring as quickly as you can.

A spring fires you high into the air. Use Homing Attacks and a midair dash to reach the distant rainbow ring.

The alley to the right is the faster path and provides a straight route to dash panels that send you flying above the crowded city streets.

Use a Homing Attack on this hapless robot to reach the awning and the item upon it.

Once you regain control of Sonic, head left and take this narrow side street to cut down your time.

Item!
An item rests on the awning, the reward for pulling off a tricky maneuver.

Four successful Homing Attacks are required to bypass the enemies at street level. When you begin running on the wall, use Quick Steps to gather a large amount of rings.

Drift through this U-turn and pull off five successful Homing Attacks to reach the rainbow rings and the upper walkway.

Right after the Wall Jump, use two Homing Attacks to reach the first red ring. The red rings will lead you into a cannon. Correctly follow the single onscreen button press to launch Sonic high into the air and through a series of red rings and a rainbow ring. You'll land on an elevated walkway that leads to a second cannon.

...ter the camera ...anges perspective, hit ...e spring and perform ...midair dash to make ...through the rainbow ...ng. If successful, you'll ...ab a zip line and ...avel down a taut rope. ...t its end, use Homing ...tacks to reach the next section.

Again, quickly and correctly follow the single button press and you'll be sent hurling through the air at top speed. Once you land, perform a series of jumps to bridge the gaps between rooftops.

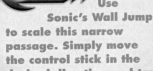**TIP**

Use Sonic's Wall Jump to scale this narrow passage. Simply move the control stick in the desired direction and tap the Jump button as you contact each wall.

NOTE

If you need more practice with the Wall Jump, play the Spagonia mission "Use the Wall Jump to Get Through!"

The high path makes navigating the towers relatively effortless. After rail-grinding down and around the second tower, use Homing Attacks to reach the zip line in the third tower.

Item!

If you're not tight on time, at the third tower, don't head forward to the next zip line. Instead, jump back and boost into the grind rail, leading you to a hidden area with an item.

After the first straightaway, take a hard right down this narrow alley. Hit the dash panel at the alley's end to send you speeding to the upper level.

An Aero-Chaser attacks Sonic once he reaches a long and straight walkway. The robot attacks with lasers and missiles. Use Quick Step to avoid the laser blasts and jump over the rocket explosions. When you get close enough, use a Homing Attack to send the metallic menace tumbling backward.

After hitting a spring, use a Lightspeed Dash to collect all the rings floating above the street and to reach the distant covered walkway.

After grabbing all the rings in the covered walkway, take a sharp left into this narrow alley. Stick to the road center to hit the dash panels and avoid hitting the walls. Once you emerge from the alley, the road widens and enough rings to fulfill your quota await you.

Whether you destroy the robot or not, you're very close to the Goal Ring. Deplete your Boost Gauge to reach it as quickly as possible.

With the tablet fragment collected, it's back to Chun-nan. Once there, visit Zonshen at the back gate and he'll express his deepest appreciation for restoring the continent. He'll also ask you to visit Hualin on the Street Bench. When you do, she'll give you the third continent's Sun Tablet. Enter the Sacred Shrine and play Chun-nan's daytime missions.

Item!

An item sits at the foot of the steps that lead to the Goal Ring. Stick to the path's center and you'll pick it up.

GATHER RINGS AT TOP SPEED!

Type	Reward(s)	Items Found	Unlocks
Daytime	Moon Medal, Tablet fragment adorned with a red jewel	—	Wall jump to get through

You have 1'30 to collect 200 rings.

Item!

Visit Chun in the restaurant to obtain Secret Soundtrack 40.

HEAD FOR THE GOAL!

Type	Reward(s)	Items Found	Unlocks
Daytime	Moon Medal(s)	Illustration 2, Illustration 12, Secret Document 10	Gather rings at top speed!

Time	Ranking	Reward
3'10'000	S	Three Moon Medals
3'40'000	A	Two Moon Medals
4'40'000	B	One Moon Medal

...tilize all that you've learned to reach the Goal Ring as quickly as possible.

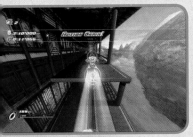

Shortly after the level begins, you'll hit a spring. Pull off three Homing Attacks to reach the upper path.

Item!

...f you do land on the center path, there is an item ...hat is dead center as you exit the building. If you ...ake the left path, be sure to play this level again ...nd get it!

...he toughest part of the ...ission is just ahead. ...he next bounce pad ...ou hit will send you ...ing through the air. ...front of you, three ...aths diverge. If you fail ...pull off any Homing ...tacks or fail to reach

...e distant red ring, you'll fall to the red wooden bridge below ...nd be forced to take the longest and slowest path. If you ...ccessfully reach the red ring, you can steer Sonic in midair to ...each the middle, paved path. However, you want to reach the ...ft path.

To reach the left path, pull off three Homing Attacks and then let Sonic fall toward the bridge. About halfway down, the first in another row of robots will be auto-targeted. Use another Homing

...ttack and you're on your way to the left path. Just three more ...oming Attacks and a midair dash will send you through the ...ainbow rings and speeding over the paved straightaway.

Once you land, Quick Step back and forth to pick up as many rings as possible. As you approach the covered portion, Quick Step to the path's far right side. You'll need to execute a Lightspeed Dash to make it over the water below.

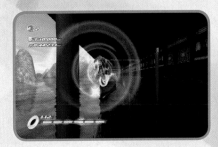

The path widens and you must Quick Step to navigate through the large crates that block your way.

As you approach the next covered section, stick to the path's left side and be prepared to execute two more Lightspeed Dashes. Afterward, a raised dash panel sends you back onto the main path.

Item!

Successfully executing the Lightspeed Dash on the path's left side will send you speeding over an item container.

Leave the main path and boost over the water here to save some time.

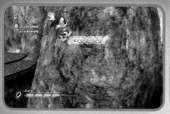

Successfully follow the series of three onscreen button presses to reach the upper path, which is faster. You'll also need to pull off a Wall Jump to remain on the upper path.

After a loop sends you careening forward, leap from the crest of the hill to make it through the series of three red rings. If you miss the rings, pull off a Homing Attack to reach the zip line; you'll lose less than a second.

More Homing Attacks keep you on the fast path. When you hit the first horizontal bar, leap off it as you spin toward the second bar. While in midair, use a Homing Attack to reach the second bar. Jumping from the second bar sends you flying to the upper path.

Whether or not you successfully navigated the horizontal bars, prepare yourself for a precision jump. A dash ramp sends you flying toward a red ring. You'll fall short of it unless you perform a midair dash at the correct time. Do so when you're exactly even with the ring, and the extra bit of distance you gain will be sufficient to send you flying through the center. Now enjoy the ride as you are sent speeding through three more red rings and a rainbow ring.

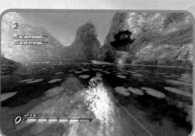

Once you land, it's time to hit the gas and use some of that Boost energy you have stored up. Quick Step around the giant spears that pierce the path in front of you and keep up the speed to hydroplane over the water area.

TIP

If you are good at hydroplaning, then there are two shortcuts that can be found in this area. After the first walkway, head to the right over the water and between the Thunder Ball robots to shave some seconds. Then, after another short bridge, hydroplane to the left into the cave to lose a lot off of your final time.

Keep your speed up throughout the next area as you dodge crates and even a rocket-firing robot. Hit a spring and you'll come to a new obstacle. These flat red rings act as trampolines, allowing Sonic to bounce from one to the next. Don't worry about jumping—you do that automatically. Just use the control stick to move Sonic forward and your momentum will carry you to the road.

Make sure you hit the center of this dash panel or you'll miss the red ring and fall to your death.

When you begin hydroplaning, stay to the right to reach an item on a small rocky plateau.

Item!

It won't cost you much time to reach this item. Just nail a few Homing Attacks, grab the goods, and continue on your way.

The Goal Ring sits just ahead in a grove of cherry trees. Boost away and enjoy the view.

GATHER RINGS AT TOP SPEED!

Type	Reward(s)	Items Found	Unlocks
Daytime	Moon Medal	—	Don't break anything along the way!

You have 1'10 to collect 200 rings.

Hit the raised dash panel and follow the three onscreen button presses to reach the upper level.

Perform a Wall Jump to reach the rail and rack up even more rings.

Jump before the path slopes downward and execute three Homing Attacks; the rest of the rings will be yours in no time.

DON'T BREAK ANYTHING ALONG THE WAY!

Type	Reward(s)	Items Found	Unlocks
Daytime	Moon Medal, tablet fragment adorned with a red jewel	—	Reach the goal unscathed

You have 2'00 to reach the goal without breaking a single jar.

Stick to the road's center or use Quick Steps to avoid the two pairs of jars.

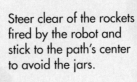

Let the trampolines do the work; just guide Sonic toward the walkway.

Steer clear of the rockets fired by the robot and stick to the path's center to avoid the jars.

To reach the road after the second set of trampolines, execute a Homing Attack against the distant robot.

The Goal Ring is close. Be quick but don't lose control. Stay to the path's right to avoid the red jars, and then stick to the center and you're home free.

Time to head back to Spagonia to visit the Pickle Lab. The professor sends you to Aqueduct Street to enlist Otto's help. He'll reunite the tablet fragments to form the second continent's Planet Tablet. There's no time to waste; use the Planet Tablet to open the Planet Door in Spagonia's Sacred Shrine.

When the perspective changes to a side-scro get ready to do some precision jumping. Mo to the screen's center and wait for the multip laser beams to ignite. Shortly, they'll all start moving clockwise. You must jump the low bea while dodging the high ones. This will take bot vertical and horizontal midair adjustments to pull off. Once you have clear shot, use a Homi Attack to send the spik ship spinning.

BOSS: EGG DEVIL RAY

Type	Reward(s)	Items Found	Unlocks
Daytime	—	—	—
Time	**Ranking**	**Reward**	
3'40'000	S	One Moon Medal	
Any time greater than 3'40 yields a "C" ranking and no Moon Medal is awarded.			

When the perspective changes to an overhead view, you must dodge laser beams and projectiles. Stay near the screen's center to give yourself ample time to react to the ship's armament. When its shields drop, Boost into it to inflict damage.

Eggman's creation greets you with laser beams from its wing-mounted cannons. Fortunately, the cannons glow just prior to firing, giving you enough time to Quick Step out of harm's way. When it drops its shield to retract its wings, Boost into it to inflict damage.

NOTE

It's imperative to keep collecting rings. Without them, you'll miss out on mos of the opportunities to damage the Devil Ray.

With the destruction of the last obstacle standing between you and the Gaia Temple, Sonic is free to restore the power of yet anoth Chaos Emerald, and in doing so, restore th second continent.

Speak to Professor Pickle for the location the next fragment.

Item!

Anytime after the fight with the Egg Devil ray, head back to Chun-nan at night and talk to Hualin at the Street Bench to receive Secret Soundtrack 41.

Item!

Visit Lucia and Ippolita on Main Street during the day to acquire Secret Soundtrack 38.

RESTORING THE FOURTH CONTINENT

Holoska

Night has fallen over the frigid region of Holoska; fortunately, our hero's nocturnal form provides perfect protection from the cold.

VILLAGE: NIGHTTIME

Location	Name	Description	Unlocks	Rewards
Family Home	Marketa	A frightened girl grateful for your company	—	Secret Soundtrack 37
Storage Area	Yari Sure	A broken father and husband who needs your support	Sacred Shrine (after speaking with Sarianna)	Fourth continent's Moon Tablet
Central Bonfire	Yari Pecca	A seemingly senile citizen	—	—
Food Storage Area	Sarianna	A guardian of the Gaia Temple	Storage Area (new dialogue)	—
Sacred Shrine	N/A	The fourth continent's Gaia Temple	—	—

Professor Pickle sends you back to the frigid village of Holoska. After visiting Sarianna and learning that she and her husband are Temple Guardians, speak to Yari at the storage area for the fourth continent's Moon Tablet. You'll need to show confidence in his character to gain the tablet, but everyone deserves a second chance, right? Once you have the tablet, use it to open the Moon Door in the Sacred Shrine.

Item!

Visit Marketa to obtain Secret Soundtrack 37.

ACT I: THE AURORA SNOWFIELDS

Type	Reward(s)	Items Found	Unlocks
Nighttime	Sun Medal	Secret Illustration 19, Secret Illustration 34, Secret Illustration 35	Act II: The Ice Floe

Ranking	Reward
S	Three Sun Medals
A	Two Sun Medals
B	One Sun Medal

Target time for this mission is six minutes.

Item!

Pick up the item nestled behind the lone igloo.

A three-hit combination will destroy these breakable ice walls.

The Dark Gaia minions that assault you in this ice cavern should fall easily to your skilled attacks. Cut them down and then grab the narrow ledge to reach the upper path.

Item!

An item sits on a tall ice pillar. To get it, jump onto the ice structures and use a Dark Bat to bridge the last gap.

Jump from Dark Bat to Dark Bat to cross the gap.

These fans have adapted quite nicely to their frigid surroundings and now blow air cold enough to freeze Sonic dead in his tracks. Shake the Remote and Nunchuck up and down to break free from your icy prison.

Item!

An item rests in a small alcove directly below the narrow ledge upon which Sonic stands. Hop down, grab it, and hitch a ride on the Dark Bat to return to the main path.

Giant snowballs careen toward Sonic. Take evasive maneuvers to avoid them and quickly but carefully make your way past them.

This battle is made a bit more difficult with the spike traps that sit beneath the thin sections of ice. Avoid the lightly colored areas and take out the enemy combatants using your full arsenal of special attacks. When necessary, grab the rings that surround the perimeter to refill your health.

After the battle, the barrier blocking the Goal Ring dissipates. Victory is yours!

ACT II: THE ICE FLOE

Type	Reward(s)	Items Found	Unlocks
Nighttime	Sun Medal	Secret Illustration 18, Secret Illustration 72, Secret Illustration 75	Act III: The Temple of Ice

Ranking	Reward
S	Three Sun Medals
A	Two Sun Medals
B	One Sun Medal

Target time for this mission is nine minutes.

Item!

After two leaping ledge-grabs, look to the left and break the ice block on the platform to make the Dark Gaia Bat appear. Hitch a ride to a small, snow-covered platform and use the glowing ledge to shimmy over to a well-hidden item. Use the Dark Bat to return to the main path.

After navigating two glowing poles, you reach an air vent blowing freezing air. Wait for the current to subside or simply hop over it to pass by safely.

Fans make this skirmish difficult. Don't get caught in their drafts or you'll freeze on the spot, leaving you vulnerable to further attack. Work your way behind the fans and destroy them first. Then concentrate on the lesser nuisances.

Item!

After navigating the two glowing poles, walk off of the pathway between the two lit torches. The platform the item is on appears on your minimap as a small offshoot from the main path.

Item!

his item equires ome kill to etrieve. Hop nto the elevated narrow walkway to the main ath's right. Leap and grab the interactive ledge, ull yourself up, turn around, and jump to the other ide. Walk down the narrow path and successfully avigate two horizontal poles. From the second ole, double-jump to the small outcropping on onic's right. Finally, leap across to reach the item.

Hop down from the ledge that held the item and turn right. Leap across the rift to the walkway beyond. Double-jump over a break in the path and climb up to the wooden scaffolding. Hug the wall as you backtrack over the wooden walkway, and make one last leap across the chasm.

If you're afraid of heights, this isn't the level for you! From your high vantage point, you can just make out the Goal Ring in the distance.

e the Dark Bat to oss to the next frozen atform. From there, p down progressively wer until you reach small divide. Leap ross it, and use two re Dark Bats to get oser to the goal.

Item!

Break the ice block on the previous platform and dash-jump to the platform with the item.

To successfully navigate this section, wait for the fan to cease blowing and then either use a wooden crate or a quick attack to defeat it.

The next fan sits on one of only two stable platforms in the area. Quickly leap to the stable platform adjacent to the fan (the platform with the crate). Pick up the crate and knock the fan into the icy waters below.

Step lightly and quickly as you cross the remaining three broken platforms. Hesitate and they'll take you down into the murky, frigid depths with them. Make it and you're one step closer to restoring the continent.

ACT III: THE TEMPLE OF ICE

Type	Reward(s)	Items Found	Unlocks
Nighttime	Sun Medal	Secret Illustration 13, Secret Illustration 39, Secret Illustration 83, tablet fragment adorned with a blue jewel	Secret Mission 6

Ranking	Reward
S	Three Sun Medals
A	Two Sun Medals
B	One Sun Medal

Target time for this mission is eight minutes.

Leap over the spike hazards and don't get caught in the frosty drafts from the ice vents.

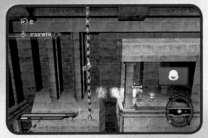

Climb this long vertica pole hanging from the ceiling, pausing only t wait for the fan's airflo to subside.

Item!

Hop down from the elevated path and claim the item sitting offscreen, directly across from the spike traps.

Leap from one pole to the next, avoiding the wall-mounted vents and the vent from the fan. Leap over the fan from the second pole and attack it from behind. Then, press the green button to raise the door

above. Hop back onto the longer pole and climb up.

After you grab the item, climb to the recessed walkway above the spike traps and step on the green button to close the ice vents above. Return to the main path and head across the gap. Step on a second green button to raise the heavy stone door.

A barrier activates as you cross the threshold into this large cavern.

Item!

Destroy the ice surrounding the item, then claim it.

SONIC
UNLEASHED™

The first Dark Energy Key is directly across from the item, against the room's left wall. Shatter the ice to obtain it.

stroy the ice to cover a low platform. p on to reach the wing ledge above. refully walk along the ntral support structure d hop onto the pillar's to reach the second rk Energy Key.

On the catwalk, avoid incoming fire by continually moving. The third Dark Energy Key sits behind the creature hovering at the screen's top.

Item!

Before dropping down, grab the item that sits atop a small pillar behind this enemy.

You meet heavy resistance upon entering the final room. Destroy the first wave with multihit combos. The second wave is comprised of floating bombs and a pair of Titans. Pick up the spikes and hurl them at the one-eyed demons or lead the spikes close to them and let the resulting explosions take 'em out.

The Goal Ring is just down one last corridor. Dash to make it under the time limit.

Head to Spagonia, where Professor Pickle will send you back to Holoska. Visit Jari-Pekka at the Central Bonfire, and he'll reveal that he's really a Temple Guardian! He also fashions a Planet Tablet from the two fragments you've collected. It's off to the Sacred Shrine to open the Planet Door.

BOSS: DARK MORAY

Type	Reward(s)	Items Found	Unlocks
Nighttime	—	—	—
Time	Ranking	Reward	
5'00'000	S	One Sun Medal	
Any time greater than 5'00 yields a "C" ranking, and no Sun Medal is awarded.			

The Dark Moray is protected by an impenetrable force field. To disable it, run around the raised circular platform and destroy all the purple power conduits.

After you destroy all the conduits, the shield falls. Quickly jump up and approach the overgrown eel and pummel the weak spot on its neck. After a few hits, frozen canisters fall to the platform behind you. Grab one and throw it at the sharp-toothed serpent. The canister will shatter, temporarily freezing your foe and leaving it open to attack. Take advantage of the situation by continually striking the eelcicle until you are forced back down to the platform's base. Repeat the entire process until the beast falls.

Once you defeat the Dark Moray, Sonic and Chip proceed to the Gaia Temple and restore the fourth continent. Return to Spagonia to learn that Professor Pickle has decided to move his laboratory to the far-off land of Shamar, which houses the next Sacred Shrine.

Meanwhile, Eggman's scheme to attract the forces of Dark Gaia to him in order to expedite the creation of his twisted fantasy land is revealed.

The beast has several attacks. It fires crystal shards down at Sonic, which remain in place for a short time and freeze Sonic when touched.

Periodically, your opponent will slam its head to the ground, and then spin, attempting to crush Sonic beneath it. After the second time the Werehog gets knocked off the platform, the Dark moray will lob icy spheres out of its mouth while the Werehog attacks the purple conduits. Avoid the attacks by constantly moving; therefore, remain stationary only when attacking, and always be ready to displace quickly.

RESTORING THE FIFTH CONTINENT
Shamar

The desert town of Shamar is a cultural center, home to a royal palace and a university.

VILLAGE: DAYTIME

Location	Name	Description	Unlocks	Rewards
Palm Tree Square	Ehsan	A gangly citizen with a stuffy nose	—	—
Back Alley	Yasmin & Zena	A pair of protective young girls	—	—
Outside the Palace	Layla	An exchange student	The Merchant's Home, Sacred Shrine	Fifth continent's Sun Tablet (after speaking with the professor)
The Merchant's Home	Assistant	Pickle's assistant has made the trip as well	Pickle Lab	—
Pickle Lab	Professor Pickle	An expert on Gaia lore	Outside the palace (new dialogue option)	—
Sacred Shrine	N/A	Fifth continent's Gaia Temple	—	—

The team packs up and moves to the desert town of Shamar. Sonic's first task is to locate the professor's new lab. Talk to Layla outside the palace, and she'll direct you to Pickle's assistant, who resides at the Merchant's Home. The assistant marks Pickle Lab on your map.

The professor has relocated Shamar's Sacred Shrine. Revisit Layla and she'll give you the fifth continent's Sun Tablet and will mark the Sacred Shrine on your map. Time to get to work!

HEAD FOR THE GOAL

When you reach the shifting sands, head to the inside of the track to reach the elevated walkway. A shortcut through the crowded streets is up ahead.

TIP

Climbing the shifting sands is easier at top speed. Try boosting to reach the high walkways.

Execute four Homing Attacks to reach the high path on the street's other side. A spring launches you through an opening in a building wall and to the street beyond.

Type	Reward(s)	Items Found	Unlocks
Daytime	Moon Medal	Secret Illustration 6, Secret Illustration 44, Secret Document 5	Land a Lightspeed Dash!

Time	Ranking	Reward
2'40'000	S	Three Moon Medals
3'10'000	A	Two Moon Medals
4'10'000	B	One Moon Medal

Utilize all that you've learned to reach the Goal Ring as quickly as you can.

Follow the trail of rings and ascend the small hill of shifting sand to reach another raised pathway. Hit the dash panel and the spring to reach the rainbow ring and pass safely over the heads of the robots below.

After ascending a hig spiral, three Homing Attacks are required keep you on the faste upper track.

Once again, shifting sands signal another high walkway. Reach it and you'll soon come to a warped bridge covered with large, spiked balls. You must run in order to navigate the obstacles safely, so keep your speed up and always stick to the outside of the track to avoid damage.

Item!

Reach the upper track to pick up this item as you speed along.

Hit a spring and execute three more Homing Attacks and a midair dash to reach a rail. It's only a quick grind session before you're thrown in the air and must once again pull off a chain of Homing Attacks and a midair dash.

Hit the dash panel to reach the undefended elevated track. Stick to the inside of the curving track to hit a dash panel.

It takes precision wall-jumping to scale the narrow space between the walls. Afterward, pull off two Homing Attacks to stay on the upper path.

Item!

The elevated track contains an item ripe for the picking. Simply stick to the path's middle to grab it without slowing down.

As you run through the canyon, stay to th right as the path splits to either side of a larg rock. Hit the spring an take to the walls. Use Quick Steps to collect the rings, and continu boosting to keep your speed up.

Once you land, veer left to travel on a narrow walkway. Hit the blue spring at the walkway's end to launch across the canyon. When prompted, you'll need to successfully execute two button presses in order to continue the express ride through the valley.

To avoid the Golden Aero-Cannons, deplete your Boost Gauge after you leave the bridge and reach the Goal Ring unharmed.

Item!

Unfortunately, you have to sacrifice time in order to grab this item. It rests in the narrow crevice between the blue bounce pad and the cliff wall. Hop down and leap over a row of spike balls to reach it.

LAND A LIGHT SPEED DASH!

Type	Reward(s)	Items Found	Unlocks
Daytime	Moon Medal	—	Gather rings at top speed!
Simply execute a Lightspeed Dash and the Moon Medal is yours.			

This row of rings sits high above the valley floor. Perform a Lightspeed Dash to gather all the rings and to travel to an area that you couldn't reach using a jump or a midair dash.

The shortcut leads to a passageway high above the lower path. Nail two Homing Attacks and then pull off a Lightspeed Dash to reach the far bounce pad. Midair-dash through the rainbow ring to land on the first of three pillars connected by a rope bridge. Hit the dash panels on top of the pillars to easily navigate the obstacle.

GATHER RINGS AT TOP SPEED!

Type	Reward(s)	Items Found	Unlocks
Daytime	Moon Medal	—	Don't break anything along the way!
You have 1'30 to grab 270 rings.			

Three Homing Attacks propel you to the upper path, which holds the most rings.

Execute a few more Homing Attacks and a midair dash to reach the rail.

After being shot through three red rings, perform four Homing Attacks and immediately execute a Lightspeed Dash to capture the most rings.

Perform three Homing Attacks here to reach the left rail. If you execute only two, you' drop onto the right rai

Next, execute a series of successful Wall Jumps to reach the upper path. Then, time two Homing Attacks to continue your trek on the high railway.

Just before the rail ends, jump up to travel through the red ring. This will send you flying over the large chasm and onto a dash panel beyond.

A fair amount of running is up next, but the jars are easily avoidable. After hitting the dash panel located in the narrow passage, be prepared to drift around a sharp corner. You have plenty of time to reach the goal, though, so don't be afraid to hit the brakes a collision is imminent.

TIP

The green hovering robots are electric. Allow them time to discharge by tapping back on the control stick to apply the brakes and then jump and perform your Homing Attacks.

Boost through the final section to pick up all 270 rings in well under one minute!

When navigating through the shifting sands, stick to the insic of the track to ensure you don't slip and bre a jar. Once you hit the final straightaway, stay left to avoid the enemi and the jars.

DON'T BREAK ANYTHING ALONG THE WAY!

Type	Reward(s)	Items Found	Unlocks
Daytime	Moon Medal	—	Gather rings at top speed!
Reach the goal in less than 1'30 without breaking anything but Eggman's robots.			

Hit the Goal Ring and add another Moon Medal to your collection.

GATHER RINGS AT TOP SPEED!

Type	Reward(s)	Items Found	Unlocks
Daytime	Moon Medal, Secret Soundtrack 8, tablet adorned with a red jewel	—	—

...ou have 1'00 to grab 70 rings.

NOTE

The name of the mission is a repeat, but the mission itself is new.

This mission is tough to fail. After a loop, you free-fall onto a trampoline. On your way up, pull off two Homing Attacks to reach the distant zip line. Once up the zip line, execute one more Homing Attacks to destroy a robot and reach a floating ring.

Item!

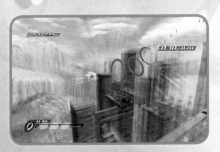

An item container rests directly in your path.

...e toughest part of ...e mission requires ...ming a midair dash ... you gain enough ...tra distance to make ...through the red ring. ...st as you line up with ...e upper section of the ...ng, dash to make it ...th room to spare.

If you correctly timed the dash, you'll hit your quota without so much as another button press! Congratulations, the tablet fragment is yours!

Back at the lab, Professor Pickle informs you that he's found yet another Gaia Temple in Adabat. However, night has fallen in Shamar, and the city is bustling with activity. Perhaps you should explore before flying to Adabat.

VILLAGE: NIGHTTIME

Location	Name	Description	Unlocks	Rewards
Palm Tree Square	Ehsan	A gangly citizen with a stuffy nose	Food Market/Sacred Shrine (after speaking with Ehran)	Fifth continent's Moon Tablet (after speaking with Ehran)
Food Market	Ehran	The son of Ehsan	Palm Tree Square (new dialogue option)	—
Outside the Palace	Layla	An exchange student	—	—
The Merchant's Home	Assistant	Pickle's assistant has made the trip as well.	—	—
Pickle Lab	Professor Pickle	An expert on Gaia lore	All locations (new dialogue options)	—
Main Thoroughfare	Musaid	An out-of-work tour guide	—	—
Sacred Shrine	N/A	The fifth continent's Gaia Temple	—	—

It appears you can postpone your trip to Adabat, as the Moon Tablet was here all along. Speak with Ehsan in Palm Tree Square and then Erhan at the Food Market. Ehran will send you right back to his father, who has the Moon Tablet; you simply need to ask for it. Time to enter the Sacred Shrine and get your Werehog on!

Required Missions

ACT 1: THE CITY OF SAND

Type	Reward(s)	Items Found	Unlocks
Nighttime	—	Secret Movie 15, Secret Illustration 46, Secret Illustration 85, Secret Illustration 86	Act II: Scorched Rock
Ranking		Reward	
S		Three Sun Medals	
A		Two Sun Medals	
B		One Sun Medal	
Target time for this mission is eight minutes.			

The enemies have grown a bit, as this first encounter illustrates. Fortunately, they're still highly susceptible to multihit combos. If the force field doesn't deactivate after you defeat the second wave, turn left and make a few jumps up to a narrow walkway that leads back over the area you were just scrapping in. Bring down a lone Dark Bat Sniper with a midair attack; with its demise, the force field dissipates.

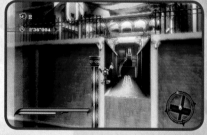

Follow the main path until you come to a ledge overlooking a narrow alley. Grab on the vertical pole and leap over to the other side.

Item!

An item sits in the alley's right corner. Drop down from the ledge to claim it, and then climb up the ladder to continue your mission.

To overcome the next encounter, pick up the floating bomb and hurl it at the Killer Bees. If that doesn't kill them, use the crates at the alley's far end.

A diverse group of enemies appear as you approach the Goal Ring, including a spike. Either grab the floating explosive and hurl it at its allies or stay away from it until it detonates and causes widespread damage. After it goes boom, clean up the leftovers with simple combination attacks.

Item!

Before leaving the area where the third encounter takes place, duck into this well-lit side corridor for an item.

Item!

Just down the main path, not far from where you picked up the last item, is another brightly lit side corridor that holds a third item.

The second wave consists of one creature, and it's all mouth. It will vomit Little Rexes from its gaping maw to nip at your heels, but don't be distracted. Focus your attacks on Big Mother and she'll go down easily; then send all the pups to that big pound in the sky. Big Mother's only real attack is a ground slam. It'll rear back, fists held high, and slam the ground with enough force to create a shock wave

...long, ornately ...ecorated courtyard is ...e setting for the next ...ncounter. Pummel the ...rge Nightmares with ...ultihit combos, and ...ecute leaping attacks to ...ke down the malevolent ...ark Bat Snipers.

with a decent radius. Jump above the wave to avoid damage and then move in for the kill. Tag the Goal Ring and put this mission behind you.

ACT II: SCORCHED ROCK

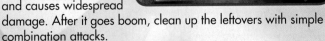

Item!

Don't take the ground-level path leading out of

...he second courtyard. Instead, leap onto the roof of ...he covered walkway (to the main path's right) and ...sneak through an elevated corridor. An item sits just ...o the left of the exit; grab it before hopping down ...o face the final encounter of this mission.

Type	Reward(s)	Items Found	Unlocks
Nighttime	Sun Medal	Secret Movie 10, Secret Illustration 45, Secret Movie 18, Secret Illustration 21	Act III: Valley of Spirits
Ranking		Reward	
S		Three Sun Medals	
A		Two Sun Medals	
B		One Sun Medal	

Target time for this mission is nine minutes.

Dash through the first section of the map, breaking jars along the way. All the jars sit on the outside of the path, so there is no need to slow down to hit them.

After the first encounter, use a glowing ledge to reach the high path. Another glowing ledge is positioned up and to the path's left. It leads through a breakable wall and to a Force Container, so skip it if you are racing against the clock.

The mission gets interesting with the introduction of a new enemy. To defeat the Flame Master, you first need to hit it with a water-filled barrel and extinguish its protective flames. Then, snuff him out with a few well-placed attacks. Use another barrel to douse the flames that block your path, and move on.

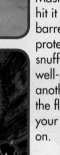

Item!

In the area after the Flame Master, there is a suspicious vertical pole leading to a seemingly empty pit. However, look for a hidden tunnel in the wall to the right of the pole that leads to an item!

By now you're familiar with climbing poles, grabbing ledges, and hitchin' rides on Dark Bats, so we'll skip to the next new addition to your long list of enemies—the Thunder Bat. Thunder Bats float high in the air and shoot balls of electricity at their prey (that's you). Get hit and you'll be momentarily stunned and vulnerable to attack, so keep moving and use the wooden crates to knock 'em outta the air.

Item!

After dispatching the Thunder Bats and other baddies, work your way to the roof of this area, then jump to the narrow wall and carefully walk the length to reach a Dark Bat and a hidden item!

Item!

 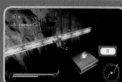

Drop from the courtyard to a small ledge below.

Run around the corner, use the interactive ledge to shimmy over to the far side, and snag the item. Return the way you came and navigate the ruins behind the structure to reach the main path.

CAUTION

Flame vents intermittently belch fire to scorch unsuspecting passersby (you again), so consider yourself warned and avoid the heat.

Big Mother strikes again, but this time he brought a friend. In such tight quarters, these two are capable of inflicting big damage with their slam attack. Attack mercilessly and continuously by opening up with a Were-Wallop and finishing with a five-attack combination. Or, use the Earthshaker if you've learned it. Once they fall, the path to the Goal Ring is clear.

Item!

This easy item is as simple as making a jump onto the small roof!

ACT III: VALLEY OF SPIRITS

Type	Reward(s)	Items Found	Unlocks
Nighttime	—	Secret Illustration 58, Secret Illustration 76, Secret Illustration 90	Act IV: Altar of Oblivion

Ranking	Reward
S	Three Sun Medals
A	Two Sun Medals
B	One Sun Medal

Target time for this mission is seven minutes.

Throw spikes to destroy the Rexes, or use Sonic's Earthshaker if they get too close.

Swing from post to post in this difficult area. From the last horizontal post, you'll need to jump in midair in order to reach the distant outcropping.

Item!

To reach the first item, jump straight up in the air from the low rock outcropping and grab the glowing ledge. Pull yourself up and use the horizontal bar to reach the item sitting atop a column.

Item!

There are two ways to reach the second item. You can jump from the column's top (where the first item sat) to the opposite valley wall. Or, you can ride the moving platform and leap from it once it passes the ledge upon which the second item sits.

Rock walls like this one can be destroyed. Some conceal hidden objects or items. In this case, it is blocking the main path. You must destroy it to proceed.

First fans, then freezing fans, and now fire fans. Don't get burned by these overgrown toasters; instead, wait for their flames to die down and then fire back with a quick combo.

CAUTION

Better late than dead, so be careful when navigating the narrow beams in this area.

Item!

Destroy the jars on the path's left side to reveal a hidden item.

Successfully navigating this spacious cavern requires careful jumping and patience. Wait until the first platform stops in front of you, and then simply walk onto it. Transferring to the second platform is just as easy—no hopping required. Grab the rings and the Force Container on the right and left pillars, respectively, or simply leap to the third platform to make better time.

Two final jumps is all it takes to reach the large rocky area where the Goal Ring is located. Unfortunately, a welcoming party waits to greet you. After you destroy the Nightmares, two club-wielding Titans materialize. You know the drill; open with a Were-Wallop and then hit 'em with multihit combinations. Keep moving or you'll be picking splinters out of your fur forever!

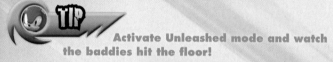

Activate Unleashed mode and watch the baddies hit the floor!

Grab rings to replenish your health and continue the fight. Once the big bruisers bite the dust, get to the Goal Ring posthaste.

ACT IV: ALTAR OF OBLIVION

Type	Reward(s)	Items Found	Unlocks
Nighttime	—	Secret Illustration 17, Secret Illustration 28, Secret Movie 11, tablet fragment adorned with a blue jewel	—

Ranking	Reward
S	Three Sun Medals
A	Two Sun Medals
B	One Sun Medal

Target time for this mission is 10 minutes.

Item!

Grab the item on the path's left, behind the breakable urns.

This large room contains six stone doors. However, only one leads to the exit. Open the second door on the right and move through the room beyond. Of the remaining five doors, two contain red Force Containers and three contain enemies.

The path splits here. Take the right path first; dodge the flame vents, and pick up the water-filled barrel. Carry the barrel down the left path, being careful to avoid the vents, and douse the flames that are blocking your way.

Dash through the next area and down the path beyond to make up some time.

Item!

When the path takes a sharp left turn, stop and approach the cliff's edge on the right. Two hops will put you on the top of a fallen column. Carefully creep along the beam to the large outcropping and turn right. Leap over the small gap and grab the item.

Once inside this room, hightail it to the water-filled barrel to get the drop on the approaching Flame Master. Hit it with the barrel to extinguish its protective flames, and then take him out. ...peat the treatment on the second Master, and then focus on ... rest of the rabble.

Item!

Climb up the broken ruins and jump up to the structure's roof. Grab on to the glowing ledge and make your way across the gap to reach the item.

Grab the iron crate and walk it up the main path until you reach a heavy door. Place the crate on the blue button to raise the door. Once you do, pillars of flame rise to block the entrance. Place the other metal crate on top of the flames, and you'll be able to pass safely by.

...ce you enter this ...om, activate Unleashed ...de and show no ...rcy. Again, the Flame ...sters should be your ... priority, as they have ...nack for disrupting ...acks.

When you've crushed the first wave, a red Titan and a red Dark Bat appear. The Titan is slow, so destroy the Dark Bat first with a simple midair attack or use the barrels. Like its blue-hued brethren, the red Titan is vulnerable from behind. However, he'll swing his club around in an attempt to knock you back. Therefore, rush in, score a few hits, and then back off. Repeat until the crimson creep perishes.

When the room is clear, the barrier drops, allowing you to reach the Goal Ring at the end of a long corridor.

Adabat is your next stop.

Adabat

Adabat is inhabited by a single family who were displaced by the recent earthquake.

VILLAGE: NIGHTTIME

Location	Name	Description	Unlocks	Rewards
Village Entrance	Nagi	A young girl	—	—
Boat House	Jamal	A hospitable teen	—	—
Central Pier	Rudi	A worried daughter who beseeches Sonic to check on her father	Sacred Shrine (after speaking to Teanchai)	Sixth continent's Moon Tablet (after speaking with Teanchai)
Shallow Waters	Teanchai	The dispirited father	Central Pier (new dialogue option)	—
Sacred Shrine	N/A	Sixth continent's Gaia Temple	—	—

The patriarch is dispirited and inconsolable, but his daughter, Rudi, is eager to lend assistance. Obtain from her the Moon Tablet and directions to the Shrine. Make haste—the nighttime missions await.

Required Missions

ACT I: STARRY NIGHT

Type	Reward(s)	Items Found	Unlocks
Nighttime	Sun Medal	Secret Illustration 22, Secret Illustration 93	Act II: Restless Coastside
Ranking	Reward		
S	Three Sun Medals		
A	Two Sun Medals		
B	One Sun Medal		
Target time for this mission is seven minutes.			

Item!

An item sits behind a breakable jar directly behind your starting location.

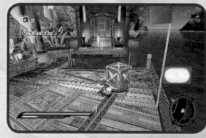

When the path splits, grab the iron crate from the left fork and carry it to the end of the right fork. Drop it onto the blue button to open the far door.

After double-jumping over two large gaps, you'll face several Frights and a Fright Master. Grab a Fright and throw it at the Master, then finish the Master before he regains his feet.

From the moving platform, grab on to the first glowing block. Then, swing over to the left block and finally to the walkway.

While swinging on the first block, grab the red Force Container by releasing the block and leaping straight up in the air.

Item!

Climb up the nearby pole and jump over to the concave ramp. An item sits on the far upper lip.

Leap from the moving platform to the glowing block. From the block, leap straight up and grab the pole. Edge around the pole until Sonic's back is facing the Dark Bat and hitch a ride to the narrow walkway.

At this point, the path splits. A Dark Bat will take you left, to a distant solitary platform that contains a red Force Container. It also requires you to defeat a large contingent of enemies before you can backtrack to the main path. Travel there only if you have the time.

Otherwise, hitch a ride a second Dark Bat directly in front of you. It will carry you to a series three horizontal poles that you must navigate successfully—or fall to your demise.

Up next are two long jumps. If you come up short, grab hold of the glowing ledges. An enemy encounter awaits you when you reach the high platform after your second jump. Finish the first wave of attackers with multihit combos, and use the iron crates to destroy the Killer Bees that comprise the second wave.

To the right of the high platform is a green pole that leads down to a blue button; press this to activate an adjacent platform. With the help of a metal crate, you can reach a floating Force Container. However, it's more trouble than it's worth, so skip the entire sequence if you aren't going for maximum Force.

This moving walkway works against you as you attempt to travel forward. Wait for the fans to finish blowing, and then either dash between them or jump over them. Turn around and destroy them before they can react and damage you. The Goal Ring is just around the corner.

ACT II: RESTLESS COASTSIDE

Type	Reward(s)	Items Found	Unlocks
Nighttime	Sun Medal	Secret Movie 16, Secret Movie 17, Secret Illustration 51, Secret Document 4, Secret Illustration 91	Act III: Deep Jungle
Ranking		Reward	
S		Three Sun Medals	
A		Two Sun Medals	
B		One Sun Medal	
Target time for this mission is seven minutes.			

Three whirlpools make crossing this lagoon hazardous to a Werehog's health. Take it slow, have patience, and you'll reach the far dock as dry as the Shamar desert.

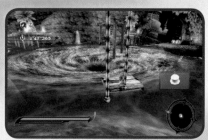

Whatever path you chose, you find yourself on the nearest of two vertical poles. Leap to the second one and slide down until you a just above the water. Turn Sonic so his back to the center of the thi whirlpool. When the third piece of debris passes underneath, drop off the pole and you'll land safely on its surface.

Carefully hop onto the first piece of driftwood. If you want to collect a red Force Container, stay on the floating debris for a trip around the eye of the whirlpool. If not, immediately hop onto the long rectangular platform.

After you hop onto the second piece of driftwood, you have another choice to make. A red Force Container floats high above the second whirlpool's center. If you must have it, hop off the plank onto the torch-lit rocky outcropping. Pull the lever, and two things will happen. First, a platform will rise up in the whirlpool's center. Second, a Dark Bat will appear. Grab on to it and it will carry you to the platform. Leap from the Dark Bat to the platform and grab the container. A second Dark Bat waits to take you to the whirlpool's other side. Grab on and then leap to a vertical pole.

Item!

An item sits on a high outcropping behind several jars. To reach it, double-jump from the wooden plank onto the outcropping. Once you have it, wait for the plank to pass below and drop onto it.

Item!

Continue riding atop the piece of wood as it makes its long circuit around the outside of the whirlpool. Leap to a concrete platform to nab another item. Wait for the makeshift raft to return and then hop on.

If that sounds like much ado about nothing, simply ride the plank until you pass the nearer of two vertical poles and then hop onto it.

The object of the next area is to reach the innermost piece of wood. To do so, leap and grab on to the glowing ledge as your raft passes beneath it. Climb up and then move to the left. Slide down the vertical pole that pierces the end of the long deck. Wait for the piece of wood to pass underneath you and drop onto it.

A Dark Bat appears above the raft. Hop up and grab on. It'll take you straight up, where two more Dark Bats await to be of service. Use them to reach the dock and put this area safely behind you.

Item!

fter getting off the dock, head to the left next to he dock. Near the water line is an item!

ce you reach the beach, other decision is required. breakable rock wall is ated on the beach's ht side. The optional ea contains an item and encounter that pits you ainst a significant force enemies, including a Mother and a pair of under Bats. It'll be a nasty t, so enter it only if you e collecting items or are ling scrappy.

If you choose to go for the item, target the Thunder Bats with midair attacks when they are not surrounded by electric barriers. Alternatively, you can hurl the Rexes at them to inflict some damage.

ve the Big Mother a wide berth to avoid the shock waves she ates, and attack fast and hard.

CAUTION

Both the Thunder Bats and the Big Mother are capable of momentarily stunning you, ensuring you'll take additional damage in the tight quarters.

Item!

The item is near the shore once you enter the cavern. Getting it is easy; getting out with it is the tricky part.

Whether you went for the item or not, you'll have to defeat a large number of enemies before the Goal Ring is accessible. Fortunately, you have a lot of room within which to operate. Unfortunately, most of the baddies have ranged attacks that stun and disorient Sonic. The name of the game is divide and conquer. Try to separate the faster moving Thunder Masters from the slower Thunder Bats. Then, use the floating bombs and quick attack combos to crush the Cretan conjurers.

Dash around the Dark Bats until they've fired their electric ordnance and then use a midair attack to cut them down. Continue moving so the other ranged damage dealers can't get a lock on you.

After the exhausting battle, claim the Goal Ring as your prize.

ACT III: DEEP JUNGLE

Type	Reward(s)	Items Found	Unlocks
Nighttime	Sun Medal	Secret Illustration 25, Secret Illustration 52, Secret Illustration 60, Secret Illustration 94	Act IV: Heavenly Ruins

Ranking	Reward
S	Three Sun Medals
A	Two Sun Medals
B	One Sun Medal

Target time for this mission is six minutes.

Item!

The item is just above and to the right of the first interactive ledge. Easy pickings for the acrobatic Werehog.

The first encounter is reminiscent of the finale to Act II. Keep moving and attack swiftly, or you'll fall prey to excessive shock treatment.

Item!

Just after the first encounter, you enter a large glade. Hop over the large tree root to nab a concealed item.

Climb the tree by using the interactive blocks as handholds. Avoid the spikes and leap up to the high natural platform.

Use the bobbers as weapons by hurling them at the firing Dark Bats; that way you'll take them out without accidentally falling off the edge.

Once the barrier falls, deftly move over the narrow branches to the series of horizontal poles. Swing, jump, and grab from one to the next to make it onto a vertical pole. From the pole, it's a short jump back onto solid ground.

Item!

Once you reach the third horizontal pole, you must jum and ignore the fourth high pole. Instead, fall toward the lower pole and grab on to it a you pass by. From there, you can leap to the area that holds the item, grab it, ar ride a Dark Bat back up.

These spike hazards block your path. However, there is just enough room to squeeze by on the nea side. Alternatively, yo can leap over them, double-jumping if necessary.

At the fork in the path, take a right to continue along the main path. Take a left if you want an item.

Item!

Getting to this item requires leaping from a pole to a ledge, a feat that by now you are accustomed to. Once you grab the item, hitch a ride on a Dark Bat that will take you all the way back to the crossroads.

If you guessed that these floating platform are unstable, you win Quickly cross from or to the next, or ride the express elevator to the forest floor.

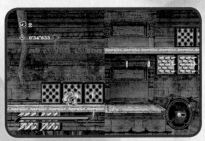

...e this moving ...tform until it passes ...ectly underneath the ...rk Bat. Hop straight ... and grab on. Wait ...il it rises and then ...p and grab on to ... green Dark Bat. Be ...tient, however; the ...een Dark Bat will intermittently burst into an electric frenzy. ...ait until it returns to normal and then make the grab.

...e final two Dark ...ts are not electric; ...wever, they are still ...ving, so glean their ...ttern before leaping ...m one to the next.

...veral baddies ...aterialize on the final ...tform in a desperate ...empt to keep you ...m the Goal Ring. ...er all you've endured ...s far, these monsters ...l prove a minor ...noyance at best. ...stroy them and grab the Goal Ring.

ACT IV: HEAVENLY RUINS

Type	Reward(s)	Items Found	Unlocks
...ghttime	Sun Medal	tablet fragment adorned with a blue jewel	—
...nking		Reward	
S		Three Sun Medals	
A		Two Sun Medals	
B		One Sun Medal	

...get time for this mission is nine minutes.

Spike hazards are set in the wall both above and below the glowing ledge. Wait until they retract and then quickly shimmy past.

CAUTION

The spikes will knock you to your death if they hit you.

You must climb up and hug the wall to get through this section. Again, wait until the spikes retract and move rapidly to the far platform.

Hang from the ledge to navigate the final section, and then leap to the vertical pole, grabbing on to it as you fall below it.

Pull the lever to activate a hanging cart. The cart briefly stops near the lever, so board it there.

Exit the cart and prepare for battle. Use the wooden crates to destroy the red Killer Bees, and then concentrate on the red Titan. Attack from the rear, and the burly beast will fall quickly.

Hop onto the hanging cart and then onto the cross-shaped central platform. Rotate the lever clockwise to move the hanging cart into position between you and the main path (which lies directly ahead). Leap from the platform to the cart and from the cart to the Dark Bats beyond.

NOTE

Position the cart to the right and left of the cross to reach two Force Containers.

Enemies appear when you reach this area. Wait for them on the big stable platform, a engage them when th approach.

Item!

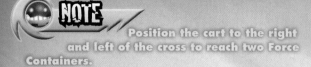

Raise the second stone door to the left of the main path to obtain an item.

This encounter is rough. Use Were-Claw attacks to stun the Thunder Masters and throw crates at the red Killer Bees. After you defeat the first wave, two blue Titans materialize. Activate Unleashed mode and take them both out.

TIP

Pick up and throw bobbers at the Masters to mitigate your risk of inadverten falling off the platform.

When it comes time to traverse the platforms, stick mainly to the dark-colored stable ones. However, you can quickly step on and off the lighter, unstable platforms before they fall away. The moss-covered areas to either side of the barrier are also a good choice for standing your ground and fighting off the rest of th Dark Gaia goons.

The path splits here. Go right for a Force Container and an item. Go left to continue along the main path. Step lightly over the lighter-colored platforms, as they are unstable and will fall away beneath your feet.

Item!

A hard-to-reach item sits high above and to the area's left. Leap from the lower of the two leftmost platforms and grab on to the hanging pole. Climb the pole and claim the item.

Item!

The item is hidden behind the structure. Walk around the near side to get it. When you return to the structure's front, you'll find a Dark Bat that will take you back to the main path. You must leap from the Dark Bat to a pole and from the pole onto a ledge.

Item!

An item is concealed behind the jars to the left of the barrier.

You've acquired the second half of the continent's Planet Tablet. Return to Pickle Lab and talk to the professor in order to unlock a new dialogue option at Palm Tree Square. Ehsan is the Temple Guardian, and he'll gladly reconstruct the Planet Tablet for you.

Item!

efore traveling to the Sacred Shrine, revisit Layla utside the palace to obtain Secret Soundtrack 43.

ead to the Sacred rine and use the anet Tablet to unlock e Planet Door.

BOSS: DARK GUARDIAN

Type	Reward(s)	Items Found	Unlocks
Nighttime	—	—	—
Time	Ranking	Reward	
5'00'000	S	One Sun Medal	

ny time greater than 5'00 yields a "C" ranking, and no Sun Medal is awarded.

e Dark Guardian has several attacks that inflict considerable amage. Its main assault is an expandable arm that it thrusts rward to answer any frontal approach. Move in cautiously d look for it to cock its arm back. Once it does, quickly uble-jump to avoid the punch, and then take a few seconds to use some damage of your own.

The green-haired grinch can close the distance very quickly with its rush attack. Keep moving or this fast attack will catch you by surprise.

close, the big but gile Guardian can rform a whirlwind tack that will daze d stun Sonic for a w seconds. When it etches its massive mmer behind it, get ay as fast as possible d keep your distance until it finishes the move.

Inflict enough damage and the Guardian teleports to a low platform, where it calls on lightning strikes to deter any approach. It is possible to navigate the strikes since the ground glows where a bolt is about to connect. When you get in close, finish a combo and then retreat; the close quarters of the platform play to the Guardian's strengths.

Its last attack is a hammer strike. It will leap into the air and bring down the massive hammer with devastating effect. When the Guardian leaps into the air, move in and take advantage of the few seconds it takes the beast to recover.

CAUTION

Don't blindly run around the arena's perimeter or you'll accidentally pick up rings that you may need later. Conserve the rings until you are badly hurt.

Once the Guardian falls, Sonic and Chip are free to refill a Chaos Emerald and restore the fifth continent. It's off once again to the professor to learn the correct course of action.

Item!

Before going to see Professor Pickle, visit the back alley during the daytime to obtain Secret Soundtrack 42.

Adabat is the location of the next Gaia Temple; time to put those frequent-flyer miles to work!

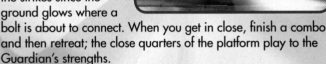

RESTORING THE SIXTH CONTINENT
Adabat

VILLAGE: DAYTIME

Location	Name	Description	Unlocks	Rewards
Village Entrance	Nagi	A young girl	—	—
Boathouse	Jamal	A hospitable teen	—	—
Central Pier	Rudi	A daughter confident in Sonic's skills	Sacred Shrine	Sixth continent's Sun Tablet
Shallow Waters	Teanchai	The dispirited father	—	—
Sacred Shrine	N/A	Sixth continent's Gaia Temple	—	—

Revisit Adabat village. Teanchai is at the Boathouse and directs you to his daughter, Rudi, who is at the Central Pier. She gives you the sixth continent's Sun Tablet in the hopes that you'll restore this continent as you did the other. Your next step is opening the Sun Door in the Sacred Shrine.

A wall divides two paths. Aim for the dash panels that sit on the path's left-hand side to guide you along the inner edge of the cliff.

HEAD FOR THE GOAL!

Type	Reward(s)	Items Found	Unlocks
Daytime	Moon Medal	Secret Illustration 7, Secret Illustration 47	Gather rings at top speed

Time	Ranking	Reward	
2'15'000	S	Three Moon Medals	
2'45'000	A	Two Moon Medals	
3'45'000	B	One Moon Medal	

Utilize all that you've learned to reach the Goal Ring as quickly as you can.

Head to the left of this cave to boost directly over the water and save some time. After you cross the water, make a sharp left to continue along the main path.

Item!

An item sits in the center of the path, near the starting line.

After a successful Homing Attack on the second robot, Sonic flies high into the air. More robots are auto-targeted over the water. Use a few more Homing Attacks and a midair dash to reach the red ring.

A spring loads you into a cannon. Once you're fired out of the cannon, follow the single onscreen button press to accelerate through a rainbow ring and reach the distant trail.

Use a Homing Attack to destroy the robot standing on the walkway's left side. This propels you upward, where you must execute two more Homing Attacks to reach a concealed upper walkway.

Four Homing Attacks and a midair dash allow you to reach a hanging vine. Leap from the hanging vine as it swings forward and jump in midair to reach the nearby ramp.

You must jump up and through the rainbow ring to activate it. Simply trying to run through will send you to a watery grave.

...ap from vine to vine ...d then to a fallen tree; ...ntinue your quest for ...igh ranking.

Item!

An item sits in the center of the elevated walkway. This is easy pickings if you hit the center of the dash panel.

...couple more Homing ...tacks and a midair ...sh allow you to reach ...e hanging zip line, ...ich transports you to ...e upper rail.

Drift around a corner and travel to the right, between the ornate heads and over the bridge. After being fired from the cannon, you'll once again be called upon to follow a button press. Respond correctly and you'll reach the far platform with ease.

Once you exit the jungle, an Aero-Chaser accosts you with shoulder-mounted missiles. Use Quick Steps and jumps to avoid the projectiles, and use dashes to get through the area as ...ickly as possible. Hit the spring at the end of the wooden ...lkway to put the iron eyesore behind you.

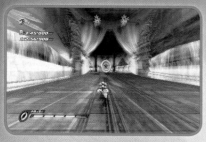

You're almost home. Drift around the remaining corners and make liberal use of Sonic's boosts to expedite your trip to the Goal Ring.

GATHER RINGS AT TOP SPEED!

Type	Reward(s)	Items Found	Unlocks
Daytime	Moon Medal	—	Time attack! Race for the goal!
You have 1'20 to collect 150 rings.			

Stick to the left of the dividing wall by hitting the dash panels that sit on the narrow path's far left.

Collect the rings on the beach and then follow them to the shoreline to the cave's left.

NOTE You have ample time to complete this level. Slow down and even turn around if you must in order to grab a majority of the rings that litter the beach.

The dash panels near the shore will send you hydroplaning over the water and over a small island that holds 20 rings. When you reach the path on the far side, turn left.

CAUTION

Keep your speed up as you cross over the water or you'll drown.

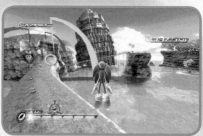

Execute a series of Homing Attacks to reach the rings that flc overhead. If you picke up a majority of the rings thus far, this will put you over the top.

TIME ATTACK! RACE FOR THE GOAL!

Type	Reward(s)	Items Found	Unlocks
Daytime	Moon Medal	Secret Soundtrack 9	Gather rings at top speed!
You have 50 seconds to reach the goal.			

NOTE Checkpoints placed throughout the level add time to your total, so finding then is imperative.

TIP  The left path is more difficult to traverse, and it saves only a few seconds, so stick right if you're having trouble.

 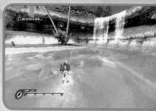

Following the shoreline rather than going through the cave is highly recommended. The small island that you speed over contains a checkpoint that extends your time by 10 seconds.

a Homing Attack
another robot to
ch a shortcut over
lagoon. You'll need
perform three more
ming Attacks and a
air dash through a
ring, but the time
ed makes it well
th the hassle.

Press the correct button
when prompted to
reach the path on the
inlet's far side. Once
on the main path, you
immediately cross
another checkpoint.

cute four Homing
acks and vine-swing
each the upper rail.
ther down the rail, a
ing will fire you into
econd vine. Make
leap to a third vine
then to the main
h and cross another
ckpoint.

Item!

Just past the
checkpoint is an
item you can't
miss, unless you
jump over it.

Destroy two rocket-firing
robots with two more
Homing Attacks, and
then dash in midair to
reach the hanging zip
line. After that, enjoy the
ride to the Goal Ring.

GATHER RINGS AT TOP SPEED!

Type	Reward(s)	Items Found	Unlocks
Daytime	Moon Medal, tablet fragment adorned with a red jewel	—	—

You have 50 seconds to collect 130 rings.

A spring launches you
to a hanging vine.
Swing forward and leap
off to reach the high
rail.

Leap from vine to
vine to the main path,
performing a series of
three Homing Attacks to
launch you into the air,
directly behind a long
line of rings. Execute a
Lightspeed Dash to grab
the rings and reach the
far rail. From there,
you'll automatically hit
dash panels and a zip
line, which will take you
over rings and fill your
quota for the level.

Teanchai is located in
the Shallow Waters.
Seek him out, and he'll
repair the sixth conti-
nent's Planet Tablet for
you. Head to the Sacred
Shrine to face Eggman's
newest weapon.

Item!

Visit Jamal at the Boathouse to obtain Secret
Soundtrack 44.

BOSS: EGG LANCER

Type	Reward(s)	Items Found	Unlocks
Daytime	—	—	—
Time	Ranking	Reward	
3'30'000	S	One Sun Medal	
Any time greater than 3'30 yields a "C" ranking, and no Sun Medal is awarded.			

The walkway ends with blue springs. After hitting them, you must follow four successive button presses to continue the pursuit. If you fail, you fall to your death and must restart the level. Succeed and you automatically score a massive hit on the Lancer.

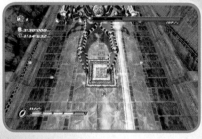

Flame pillars erupt from missiles fired by the Lancer. Use Quick Steps to avoid getting burned.

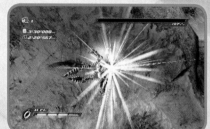

The level progression repeats until you take down the mechanical monstrosity.

When the perspective changes to a top-down view, you must move up, down, left, and right to avoid the lasers that crisscross the bridge. At the same time, gather as many rings as you can.

After the bridge, the landscape will become rocky. The Egg Lancer strikes the ground, causing boulders to fall from the top of the screen. Avoid them; when the Lancer opens its pincers, boost into the cockpit to inflict damage.

The sixth Gaia Temple restores the continent, but it also holds the secret to Chip's true identity. Chip is the Light Gaia, the champion of light. His job is to eternally protect the planet from Dark Gaia's influence. Chip is extremely grateful for Sonic's friendship, but they still have one last adventure to undertake. Visit the professor in Shamar to learn the location of Eggman and his terribly twisted creation.

Item!

Before meeting the professor, revisit Adabat at nighttime. See Nagi at the village entrance for Secret Soundtrack 45.

During this long straightaway, you must avoid the Lancer's beams and simultaneously dodge the projectiles fired in a fan pattern. Stick to the screen's center to give yourself enough time to react. When the pincers are open wide, boost into the cockpit to knock your foe back.

Tell the professor you are ready to go, and you'll automatically arrive in Eggman Land, the mechanized malevolent midway created through Eggman's exploitation Dark Gaia's powers.

Eggmanland

HEAD FOR THE GOAL!

Type	Reward(s)	Items Found	Unlocks
Daytime	Moon Medal	Secret Illustration 8, Secret Illustration 10	Gather rings at top speed!

Time	Ranking	Reward
4'30'000	S	Three Moon Medals
5'00'000	A	Two Moon Medals
6'00'000	B	One Moon Medal

...lize all that you've learned to reach the Goal Ring as quickly as you can.

After dodging the giant spiked balls, leap off the track's edge and perform two Homing Attacks and a Lightspeed Dash to navigate a shortcut.

Aim for the dash panels and drift around the sharp corners.

...ep your speed up ...you traverse this ...rped bridge and hit ...e spring at its end. ...ecute Homing Attacks ...nter Eggmanland.

Perform a Homing Attack to reach a cage in the Eggman Ferris wheel. Wait until the Ferris wheel begins its ascent, and then leap from the cage and execute a Homing Attack against the first of three hovering robots. Repeat the Homing Attacks until a zip line sends you onto a high rail.

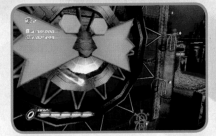

Item!

Stick to the path's center to nab this item, which is guarded by a trio of Eggman's robots. As soon as you retrieve them item, jump up to dodge the electric robot.

Right after you start grinding, avoid this decoy rainbow ring. It'll send you back to the slower track, costing you valuable time.

Use a Sonic Boost to crush these robots, and hit the dash panel they are standing on.

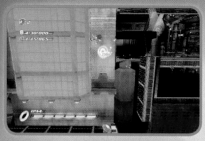

Shortly after you leave the lighted track, you must pull off a series of Wall Jumps. Fail and you fall to your death.

Inside the factory, the perspective changes to side-scroller. Slide beneath a hanging structure and then perform a Wall Jump stay on track.

Once you gain control of the cart, steer to the track's left to hit the first dash panel. Succeed and it'll take only minor corrections to keep the cart on the track and aimed at the dash panels. Overcompensate and you'll fly off the path.

A zip line drops you down and over a bed of spikes. Leap from the line and onto the track. Run forward and hit the blue springs. Follow two successive button presses and you'll be fired through rainbow rings and onto another zip line. Leap from the zip line and target two robots with Homing Attacks to reach the walkway.

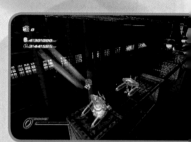

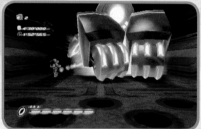

Your next challenge is to avoid the Interceptor. Don't stray too close to the track's outer edges or you'll miss the springs at the end of each section of road.

After a couple more Homing Attacks, you must slide into a low crawl space. On the other side, a spring will launch you onto a dash panel and then a zip line. The zip line lowers you next to a small rocket. Hop into the cockpit and the rocket takes flight.

NOTE

At times during the lengthy battle, Quick Steps are the only way to control Sonic.

Once you destroy the Interceptor by using the familiar tactic of Quick Stepping to the side of its attacks only to unleash the Sonic Dash against it, you'll be bounced around a lava-filled room. Execute three Homing Attacks to continue the race. Afterward, be prepared to pull off a Lightspeed Dash to reach the track.

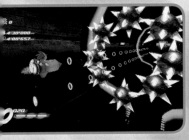

As the rocket zips along, move it up and down to collect the rings. Before long, you'll need to steer it through the center of a ring of spikes. Shortly thereafter, position the rocket so it hits the brown door. The rocket will explode on impact and fling Sonic through the hole and back onto the track.

At the pipe's end, a raised dash panel fires you into the air. When you land, run forward, between two robots, to hit the next panel. The next time you land, a robot falls right in your path. Boost through him, run to the side of him, or use a Homing Attack to destroy him and then hit the next dash panel.

r a long aightaway, drift und a sharp right n and speed by a trio Mole Cannons.

Four robots greet you on the final platform. Run in between them and hit the spring. In the air, reach the rainbow ring by destroying the Electro-Spinner with a Homing Attack.

This severely warped bridge will cause you a lot of grief if you don't navigate it at high speed. Aim for the dash panels on the outside of the track to keep you in line; they'll correct your trajectory and fire you the next dash panel. Hit them all and you'll reach the end h little hassle.

Quick Step in the direction indicated by these lighted signs—first left and then right.

o Egg Launchers ait you after your trip er the bridge. Keep to outside of the large e you're running p to avoid them mpletely, or leap up d destroy them with ming Attacks.

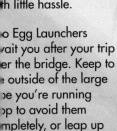

Target the parallel bar after a spring launches you into the air. Use your momentum to execute two Homing Attacks and reach the track below. After you land, Quick Step either right or left to avoid the hole in the track's center.

Item!

An item sits in the path's center, just after you are forced to Quick Step either left or right. Slow down and pick it up.

After hitting two springs, execute two Homing attacks and a midair dash to pass through a rainbow ring. Target and hit another spring and you'll face two more parallel bars. Bars are just like any other object, so target them with Homing Attacks to reach them.

Weave a path betwe[en] the spike hazards to quickly add to your r[ing] total.

After leaping from the second bar, execute a Homing Attack and a Lightspeed Dash to safely return to the track. From there, it's a short run to the Goal Ring.

After you pass the Ferris wheel, you can target four robots with Homing Attacks to reach the high rail. However, reaching the more lucrative path requires that you pull off only three attacks. After destroying the first airborne robot, fall straight down. You'll pick up a line of rings and hit a trampoline that will catapult you high into the air and over to a rail.

GATHER RINGS AT TOP SPEED!

Type	Reward(s)	Items Found	Unlocks
Nighttime	Moon Medal	Secret Soundtrack 10	Time Attack! Race for the goal!

Time	Reward
1'00'000	1 Moon Medal

You must collect 280 rings in two minutes.

After a short rail grind, execute three Homing Attacks and [a] Lightspeed Dash and you'll enter a cart.

Use a Homing Attack and a Lightspeed Dash to gather the rings floating above the track.

Take the left path to collect the most rings. Use a Sonic Dash to destroy the robot guards.

Item!

Once you enter the cart, no additional effort is required to obtain this item.

...en you gain control ...he cart, make only ...or adjustments or ...'ll fly over the edge. ...n for the dash panels ...ated on the track's ...side edge, and they'll ...p your path true. Hit ...center of the panels ...d you'll collect enough rings to fulfill your quota.

TIME ATTACK! RACE FOR THE GOAL!

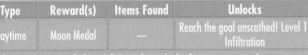

Type	Reward(s)	Items Found	Unlocks
...aytime	Moon Medal	—	Reach the goal unscathed! Level 1: Infiltration

...have 2'10 to reach the goal. Pass through checkpoints to extend your time.

NOTE

Refer to the prior mission, "Head for the goal!" for a step-by-step walkthrough, as the critical path is the same. Included here are the locations of each checkpoint.

The first checkpoint sits at the end of the left path. Simultaneously dispatch the robots and make up time by using a Sonic Dash to reach it.

...er using Homing ...acks and a ...htspeed Dash to ...vigate a midair ...ortcut, hit the dash ...nel to send you ...eening through a ...eckpoint.

Every possible path leads to Sonic behind the wheel of a coaster cart. At the end of your joyride, a dash panel sends you, sans cart, through another checkpoint.

The fourth checkpoint sits in the track's center during Sonic's first opportunity to attack the Interceptor. Stay in the middle of the road or lose an opportunity to gain more time.

After you destroy the Interceptor, Sonic is thrown around the perimeter of a lava-filled room. Perform a Lightspeed Dash to return to the track and earn another checkpoint.

After sliding under a low-hanging wall, perform a Wall Jump to reach the top track and another checkpoint.

Several successful Homing Attacks keep you on the high road. Your reward is another checkpoint.

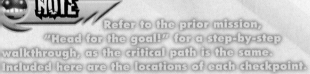

The destruction of the forthcoming rocket sends you speeding down a red rail. Lay off the controls and let the dash panels send you hurling through another checkpoint. It's the last one for quite some time, so make sure you hit it.

Breaking another door on the hall's right side leads you to the level's first encounter.

The next checkpoint sits just to the left of the sign that warns of the hole in the path's center. Just a bit past it, on the track's opposite side, is the final checkpoint. After passing through it, there are no more time extensions available.

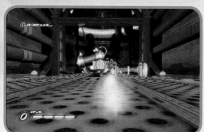

Item!

Hop onto the metal crate and then atop the machine to reach a green button. Step on it and a door will rise across the room, revealing an item. To reach the item, grab the glowing ledge, pull yourself up, and then shimmy along it to the small alcove containing the item.

To cross this large divide, wait until the vents cease blowing and then leap across the chasm. The wall on the other side sports fixtures that Sonic can grab on to, much like Spinning Poles. Grab on to the first one and then swing over to the next. Finally, leap to the nearby walkway.

LEVEL 18
INFILTRATION

Type	Reward(s)	Items Found	Unlocks
Nighttime	Sun Medal	Secret Illustration 48, Secret Illustration 49, Secret Movie 20	Level 2: Robot Factory

Ranking	Reward
S	Three Sun Medals
A	Two Sun Medals
B	One Sun Medal

Target time for this mission is seven minutes.

Stepping on a green button opens a door to this large circular elevator. Just to ensure your descent isn't boring, plenty of enemies materialize to keep you company.

Item!

Break the door at the end of the first long corridor to continue your infiltration of Eggmanland.

Leap from the elevator floor to this raised alcove. An item sits inside, obscured by wooden crates.

Item!

n the hall after the elevator there is a hard-to-
each ledge on the right. Use a box to jump up and
grab it.

After you leave the elevator, follow the corridor to an apparent dead end. However, the floor beneath your feet is breakable. Pull off a Were-Hammer to reach the path below.

Big Mother and her onies greet you on a rge grated platform.

LEVEL 2: ROBOT FACTORY

Type	Reward(s)	Items Found	Unlocks
ighttime	Sun Medal	Secret Illustration 50, Secret Illustration 54, Secret Movie 21	Level 3: Beyond the Factory

Ranking	Reward
S	Three Sun Medals
A	Two Sun Medals
B	One Sun Medal

arget time for this mission is eight minutes.

After defeating a large force of enemies, you come to a pair of moving treadmills. Moving against the treadmill's motion is tough, but you can do it by jumping or dashing. That said, leap over the first treadmill and onto the one beyond it.

The next treadmill will force you into spikes if you don't act quickly. Continually leap to the left to make progress.

Flames erupt from the wall vents and block your tedious movement over the treadmills. Wait for them to recede and then dash or jump past them.

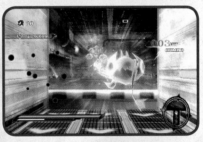

Destroy the three Thunder Bats with midair attacks, and the barrier will drop, allowing you to continue your journey.

Two Flame Masters and a host of other creatures attempt to end your mission. Focus on the fire-throwers first by dousing them with water-filled barrels, and then squash the less-threatening baddies.

Extinguish the flames with a water-filled barrel to access the interactive block above. Grab the block and fling yourself up and onto the high walkway.

Turn right to step onto the perpendicular narrow treadmill. Nea its end, turn to Sonic's left to move onto yet another treadmill. The treadmill passes benea a shower of flames, bu the iron crate you are carrying protects you from harm.

Item!

While hanging from the interactive block, fling yourself right to reach a narrow, elevated catwalk. An item sits at its far end.

Move against this treadmill's movement to the far side. Step on the green button and the treadmill's direction will reverse. Grab the water-filled barrel, carry it over the treadmill, and throw it at the flames that block your progress.

Immediately after leaving the treadmill, a group of foes accosts you. Use the iron crate to smash the flying fiends, and good ol' combinations take care of the rest.

Item!

An item sits at the foot of the first treadmill, just below your elevated position. Drop down to collect it.

When the battle is over, use the interactive blocks to reach the Go Ring that sits on the hig walkway. Your last leap requires you to grab on to a glowing ledge. Once you do, shimmy to the right to avoid the spikes and then pull yourself up.

Follow the first treadmill to its terminus at a small platform. Then, step on the green button to reverse its direction. Grab an iron crate and walk it down the treadmill.

Item!

After clearing out the enemies, use the iron crate to reach a grab ledge to the left. On top is a platform with an item.

LEVEL 3: BEYOND THE FACTORY

Type	Reward(s)	Items Found	Unlocks
Nighttime	Sun Medal	Secret Illustration 31, Secret Illustration 55, Secret Document 8	Level 4: To Zero Point
Ranking		Reward	
S		Three Sun Medals	
A		Two Sun Medals	
B		One Sun Medal	

Target time for this mission is seven minutes.

Leap from the end of the platform to the glowing pole. Once it's firmly in your grasp, slide down until the adjacent pole is in sight.

Leap to the second pole and grab on tight. Climb to its top and jump to the nearby horizontal pole. Two more acrobatic leaps and you'll reach a narrow walkway.

Large blocks move over the walkway and then recede into deep alcoves. Wait until the first one recedes and then quickly continue along the path. You must destroy the Killer Bees that appear without letting the blocks push you off the walkway.

Item!

After you destroy the Killer Bees, turn around and leap from the step onto the top of the first block. From there, you can leap from the block to reach the floating item.

From the top of the first block, leap to the top of the second block and so on until you reach the elevated path.

A long block provides passage to a hanging pole, but be careful—it also recedes. Wait until it pops out and then quickly hop onto it and run to its far side. Make a grab for the pole before you lose your footing.

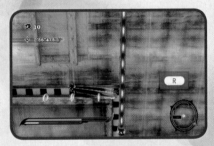

From the vertical pole, leap from horizontal pole to horizontal pole. From the fourth horizontal pole, leap and grab on to a glowing ledge. Pull yourself up and continue your assault on the madman's obstacle course.

NOTE

This view can be intimidating and disheartening, but rely on your skills and you'll make it through.

Transfer from one platform to another and then hop onto a hanging, glowing pole. From there, leap onto a third platform.

Repeat the process u[ntil] you end up on a narr[ow] ledge. At the ledge's end sits the second D[ark] Energy Key.

From the third platform, grab the interactive block and hang on. When the spikes recede, fling yourself to the next block.

Backtrack to the glowing pole and slide to the bottom. Leap from it to the glowing ledge and then shimmy around to the ledge's other side.

Item!

From the second interactive block, hurl yourself straight up to reach a floating item. Don't forget to grab the block on your way back down!

Item!

Continue shimmying along the glowing ledge until you reach a small hidden alcove. Drop down to grab the item.

From the third block, leap onto a moving platform by releasing your grip and pushing right on the control stick. Ride the platform to the walkway and nab the first Dark Energy Key.

Climb onto the yellow ledge and then reach out and grab the horizontal pole. Cross from pole to pole until you reach another purple pole. Slide down until the adjacent pole comes into view and then leap to it.

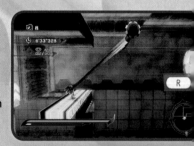

Leap from pole to Da[rk] Bat to ledge and pull yourself up. Up the p[ole] lies the third and fina[l] Dark Energy Key. Gr[ab] it and move close to t[he] barrier to deactivate [it.]

Jump from the multi-colored walkway onto a glowing pole. Position yourself on the pole so that you are just above the walkway. Leap from the pole to the interactive block protruding from the wall.

Past the barrier is another circular eleva[tor] platform. Fight your way to the bottom an[d] claim the Goal Ring.

BOTTOM LEVEL: DARK GAIA CAULDRON

Type	Reward(s)	Items Found	Unlocks
Nighttime	Sun Medal	Secret Illustration 5, Secret Illustration 36, Secret Illustration 80, Secret Illustration 71	Boss — Egg Dragoon

Ranking	Reward
S	Three Sun Medals
A	Two Sun Medals
B	One Sun Medal

Target time for this mission is eleven minutes.

Item!

Right at the start, look up to see a glowing ledge above. Jump to reach it. After some easy jumping, there is an item on a high alcove to the right.

Destroy two breakable doors to continue your quest to reach the Gaia Temple, and then grab on to the glowing pole.

Item!

Climb up the pole to reach a hidden area that contains an item and a Force Container.

Climb down and release the pole, and the action heats up. The water-filled barrels are great weapons against the Flame Masters; afterward, use them to douse the flames that prevent you from reaching the Thunder Bats.

Item!

Once you enter a large lava-filled room, hop down a small step and destroy crates to reveal a hidden item.

Climb up a pole and leap to a grated walkway. Ascend the ramp and a barrier rises, signaling another encounter. Dash and double-jump across the divide, and wage war against the latest batch of expendable foot soldiers.

Three Dark Bats await to lead you to your next destination—a meeting with a Titan. After you put down the one-eyed freak by attacking it relentlessly, use one last Dark Bat to reach the next walkway. After an easy jump, go left at the door and proceed into the next room.

Item!

Head down the walkway to find this item.

Descend a pole and a ramp, then leap to this glowing ledge.

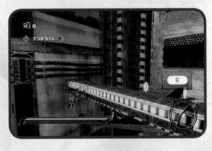

After leaping a gap, carefully traversing narrow catwalks, and descending a pole, you come to a wall decorated with receding spikes. They appear too quickly to simply run in front of, so you must double-jump over each group.

Grab the first interactive block and fling yourself from one to the next. Once you are hanging from the third block, release your grip and turn away from the wall. While you're falling, grab on to the nearby pole and haul yourself in. Slide to the pole's bottom and make the short jump to the nearby platform. Destroy the breakable wall and proceed down the corridor beyond.

Gaia troops materialize to make you earn the Goal Ring. Use Were-Wallops and combination attacks to obliterate the first wave, and focus on the Thunder Masters during the second wave. Finally, a Titan rises to introduce you to his club. Move to the oaf's blind side and let him have it with combination attacks.

Sonic and Chip arrive at the final Gaia Temple and renew the last Chaos Emerald's power. All appears well, until Eggman arrives to unleash his latest creation.

BOSS: EGG DRAGOON

Type	Reward(s)	Items Found	Unlocks
Nighttime	—	—	—
Time	Ranking	Reward	
7'00'000	S	One Sun Medal	
Any time greater than 7'0 yields a "C" ranking and no Sun Medal is awarded.			

As the earth beneath Sonic's feet falls ever farther, Eggman's prototype attacks from the perimeter. First, it launches crystals from its right hand that inflict damage and knock you down. It's left hand is a Gatling gun capable of firing multiple projectiles in speedy succession.

NOTE

You cannot fall off the platform, so be brazen in your attacks and fearless in your evasive maneuvers.

Dash around the arena to avoid both attacks. If you keep moving, the odds of getting hit are drastically reduced.

Whenever the robotic pest exposes its glowing chest, rush to the outside of the arena and hit it with a midair attack. Succeed and the machine's propulsion weakens, allowing you to connect with more attacks without jumping. Perform a four-hit combination and end with an Earthshaker. You should be able to rack up an 11-hit combination every time.

SONIC UNLEASHED™

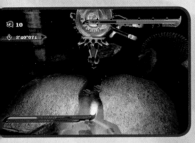

Inflict enough damage and the robot cleaves the falling platform in two, causing you to fall to a smaller platform. On your way down, steer Sonic into the rows of rings to partially refill his health.

Once you get used to them, Dark Gaia's attacks are easy to avoid. It will telegraph both of its punches, giving you time to react accordingly. All you have to do is move the control stick in the direction the punch is coming from. For example, if the punch is coming from the left, move the control stick left.

Continue to perform the 11-hit combos and the prototype will never make it to the assembly line.

With the destruction of his latest "super" weapon, Eggman is understandably upset. However, things are about to get a lot worse for our intrepid adventurers, as the now-mature Dark Gaia rises to take on the Light Gaia and his furry friend.

To strike back, simply land a punch before Dark Gaia raises its guard.

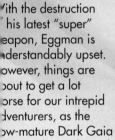

Outsized but not outmatched, Chip calls upon the power of the Gaia Temples to even the odds.

Often, Dark Gaia attacks with fierce combinations. You'll need to react quickly to successfully avoid the barrage of punches. Take advantage of any pause between its attacks to respond with a punch of your own. Time it correctly and you'll pull off a counterattack, which deals significantly more damage than the average punch. Successful timing requires shaking the Wii Remote or Nunchuck just as you finish your dodge, so there's little delay between the dodge and the counterattack.

BOSS: DARK GAIA

Type	Reward(s)	Items Found	Unlocks
Daytime	—	—	—

Time	Ranking	Reward
7'30'000	S	One Moon Medal

Any time greater than 7'30 yields a "C" ranking, and no Moon Medal is awarded.

Once and while, Dark Gaia attempts to grapple with you. If you don't pull the control stick back in time to avoid its grasp, you'll need to follow the onscreen prompt in a last attempt to break free. Throw a two-handed attack by shaking the Wii Remote and Nunchuck at the same time.

TIP

Stick to single punches to defeat Dark Gaia, as the double-punch is too slow to be effective.

The final punch sends Gaia reeling, but he isn't through yet. In a last-ditch effort to survive, he grasps the Gaia Colossus with his massive claws. It's now Sonic's turn to get into the action!

Sonic must navigate the ruins of the Gaia Temple, avoiding Dark Gaia's tendrils and attacks along the way.

BOSS: DARK GAIA CONTINUED

Hit the first glowing ramp an it's off to the races. Dodge Dark Gaia's Dark Energy Blasts by leaping over the impact zone.

Once you begin grinding, follow the onscreen prompt to jump from rail to rail and avoid obstacles. Back on the ground, leap over the Gaia tendril to avoid damage.

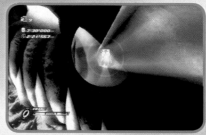

The next glowing ramp sends you flying toward Dark Gaia's exposed eye. You must successfully follow three onscreen button presses to damage the eye and move on.

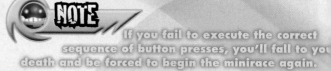

NOTE

If you fail to execute the correct sequence of button presses, you'll fall to your death and be forced to begin the minirace again.

On your way to the second eye, leap off the ramp and into the floating red ring.

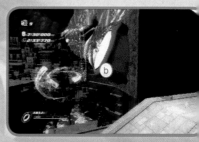

After a loop, a blue spring sends you flying. Perform the correct button press to continue along the less dangerous route.

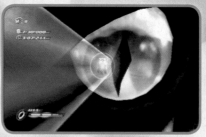

The final straightaway contains Gaia bombs. Jump over them or avoid them and concentrate on hitting the glowing ramp.

Execute three more button presses and you'll blind the second eye.

The path to the third eye is a little more difficult. When you begin, aim for the glowing ramp on the track's right side. It'll send you through a rainbow ring, which will make the race a bit easier. Once you land, be prepared to leap through a second rainbow ring located at the end of the high walkway.

The main road is fraught with obstacles, including Dark Energy Blasts and tendrils. Jumping over both hazards is highly advisable.

NOTE

Collecting rings during the run in not about adding energy to your Boost Gauge. Rather, it's about being able to take a hit without dying.

A large tendril splits the path here, but both ramps lead to the same place.

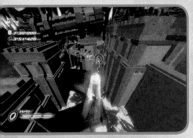

Homing Attacks are required here in order to avoid falling to your death. After the third homing attack, execute a Lightspeed Dash to make it back onto the road.

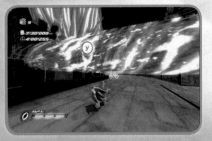

After leaping over more Dark Gaia obstacles, you'll be prompted to slide under a low-hanging tendril. Afterward, you must navigate tilting platforms. Remember, the name of the game is survival, not speed. Be quick but controlled.

CAUTION

There are no checkpoints in these races, so if you die, you begin again at the start of the current level.

This is it! Hit the ramp at the end of the final straightaway and concentrate on executing the correct trio of button presses. Do so and the Dark Gaia's grip on the colossus is weakened.

Dark Gaia is not finished yet, and it'll take more than simple Homing Attacks to put it down for good. With all other options exhausted, Sonic uses the power in the Chaos Emeralds to transform into Super Sonic. The final battle begins now.

BOSS: DARK GAIA, PERFECT

This battle is lengthy and tough. You need to move around the screen, collecting rings to fill up your Boost Gauge and dodging Dark Gaia's attacks.

While you're collecting rings, you must avoid Dark Gaia's claw attack. As the beast cocks its arm back, a faint slash flashes onscreen, illustrating where the attack will land. The faint slash is followed quickly by the actual attack. If you're wounded, you lose the majority of the rings you've collected thus far.

Collect enough rings and when prompted, perform the Super Sonic Boost. As you speed toward the main goal of reaching the eye, dodge the floating debris. If successful, you wound the eye and start the process over again. As you defeat more and more eyes, you must move around the screen to target the remaining ones. Move in the direction of the still-open eye, and when it's in front of you, the onscreen attack prompt will appear.

Once you destroy all six eyes, Dark Gaia reveals a seventh, much larger eye. Fly to the screen's edge until the eye is directly in front of you. If you have enough rings, you're prompted to make one final Boost to put Dark Gaia down for good. Be aware that the rocks come flying at Sonic faster than ever, and you must have fast reflexes to dodge them all. Try to anticipate their trajectory and maneuver accordingly. When you strike the eye, Dark Gaia is finally banished.

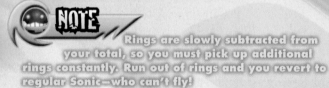

> **NOTE**
> Rings are slowly subtracted from your total, so you must pick up additional rings constantly. Run out of rings and you revert to regular Sonic—who can't fly!

When Dark Gaia gets sufficiently peeved at Sonic's constant attempts to blind him, he'll pull out all the stops and attack with all six claws simultaneously. Quickly move to the screen's center to avoid the attack.

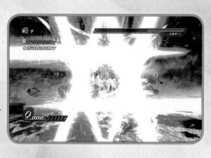

With Dark Gaia defeated, light returns to the world, and the seventh continent is restored. On every continent and in every city, the people begin rejoicing.

Eggman's plans for world domination have once again been thwarted, but whether his tenacity and ambition have been lost remain to be seen.

After you destroy a number of Dark Gaia's eyes, he'll fire projectiles of energy at you. Follow the onscreen button press at just the right moment to deflect the shot back at the source. The energy will temporarily stun Dark Gaia, allowing you to collect rings and target his remaining eyes.

Chip has returned to his ages-long slumber as well, but his friendship with Sonic will always be remembered.

OPTIONAL MISSIONS
Apotos

REACH THE GOAL UNSCATHED!

Type	Reward(s)	Unlocked by
Daytime	Moon Medal	Completing Gather Rings at Top Speed

Reach the Goal Ring in 2'30 without taking damage.

As soon as you start running, an Interceptor closes in. Wait for to slam its arms into the cobblestoned street and then move appropriately. If its arms are together, Quick Step to either side the street. If its arms are apart, stick to the middle of the street.

You can take the offensive when you find yourself trailing the Interceptor. However, save the energy in your Boost Gauge and instead focus on collecting rings.

When the Interceptor on the offensive, use Sonic's Boost to quickly reach the distant spring and escape before the can has a chance to attack.

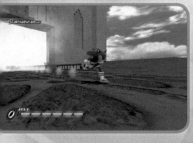

Repeat this until you reach the Goal Ring.

NOTE

Offensive-minded players can choose to destroy the Interceptor, but denying it chances to attack through effective use of the Boost Gauge is similarly gratifying.

GATHER RINGS AT TOP SPEED!

Type	Reward(s)	Unlocked by
Daytime	Moon Medal	Item Bubble in Gaia Gate

Collect 100 rings!

Grab the rings along the cobblestone path and hit the dash panel to pick up speed before entering the tunnel.

Chain attack the enemies at the tunnel's exit to gain access to the elevated walkway. Lightspeed Dash across the gap to hit the dash panel on the other side. Head right at the oncoming fork.

Grab the rings down this narrow alley, hitting the dash panel along the way.

TIME ATTACK! RACE FOR THE GOAL!

Type	Reward(s)	Unlocked by
Daytime	Moon Medal, Secret Soundtrack 13	Item Bubble in Gaia Gate
Reach the Goal Ring within the time limit. Pass through check points to extend your time.		

Jump to avoid this sho[rt] wall and use a Homing Attack to reach the spring.

Drift around the turns and hit a dash panel to speed through the first checkpoint.

After a short rail grind, slide beneath two walls to maintain your speed.

Two successful Homing Attacks send you spinning onto a blue awning. Hit the spring at its end to reach the far elevated walkway.

Three Homing Attacks will put you on the high rail, just where you want to be. Shortly after, four more Homing Attacks will allow you [to] reach a zip line.

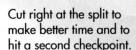

Cut right at the split to make better time and to hit a second checkpoint.

After descending the spiral path around the windmill, you'll need to quickly mimic three onscreen button presses to reach the high path and a fourth checkpoint.

When the narrow walkway bends to the left, stay on the path and be sure to hit the spring at the walkway's end. It will send you onto a blue awning. Run down the awning and jump up and through the rainbow ring, which will send you flying over the streets. Once you land, a third checkpoint is just a few steps ahead.

Jump up and through the first red ring to be launched high above the lower, and slower, path.

Item!

Hit that high red ring and this item is yours.

Use a Sonic Dash to blow away the trio of defenseless robots.

...ost through the town ...ting dash panels ...d using drifts around ...arp corners. Then, hit ...e spring and execute ...ming Attacks and ...idair dash to fly ...ough the rainbow ...g.

After you come out of a hard right turn, aim for the ascending pathway on the right. Dash panels will speed you along an elevated shortcut. When the upper path meets the lower path, the Goal ...g is just ahead. Deplete your Boost Gauge and finish ...ong.

LET 'EM HAVE IT WITH THE BEATDOWN!

Type	Reward(s)	Unlocked by
Nighttime	Sun Medal	Collecting enough Force to unlock the Beatdown ability
...t your new ability to the test.		

Perform one Beatdown to complete the mission. The Beatdown is a highly effective attack against elusive enemies. Grab 'em and then slam 'em down!

TIP

Open with a Were-Claw to stun enemies that are immune to grabs.

PREEMPTIVE STRIKE! WERE-CLAW

Type	Reward(s)	Unlocked by
Nighttime	Sun Medal	Collecting enough Force to unlock the Were-Claw ability
Put your new ability to the test.		

The Were-Claw is a quick dash attack that stuns enemies. Perform one Were-Claw to complete the mission.

TAKE FLIGHT WITH THE WERE-WALLOP!

Type	Reward(s)	Unlocked by
Nighttime	Sun Medal	Collecting enough Force to unlock the Were-Wallop ability
Put your new ability to the test.		

The Were-Wallop is a great opening attack that does damage and knocks opponents down. Perform one Were-Wallop to complete the mission.

NOTE

Foes previously hit by a Were-Wallop sustain additional damage with each subsequent attack.

UNLEASH THE ULTIMATE EARTHSHAKER!

Type	Reward(s)	Unlocked by
Nighttime	Sun Medal	Collecting enough Force to unlock the Earthshaker ability
Put your new ability to the test.		

The Earthshaker is a great finishing move that does damage to all nearby enemies. Perform one Earthshaker to complete the mission.

STRING ALONG AN EVEN BIGGER COMBO!

Type	Reward(s)	Unlocked by
Nighttime	Sun Medal	Collecting enough Force to unlock the "Combo Level Up" ability
Put your new ability to the test.		

The five-hit combination is your bread and butter. It damages multiple enemies, and what it doesn't kill outright, it stuns, leaving them vulnerable to further attack.

BE UNSTOPPABLE IN UNLEASHED MODE!

Type	Reward(s)	Unlocked by
Nighttime	Sun Medal	Completing Apotos Night Act III
Put your new ability to the test.		

You have one minute to destroy all the enemies in the courtyard. Activate Unleashed mode and have at 'em. Five-hit combination attacks work extremely well, but try mixing it up with an Unleashed-specific attack like a Tornado or a Were-Whirl.

TIP

Grab the Force container to extend the duration of Unleashed mode.

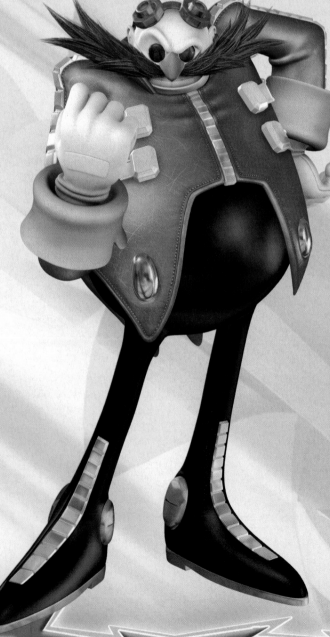

Holoska

TIME ATTACK! RACE FOR THE GOAL!

Type	Reward(s)	Unlocked by
Daytime	Moon Medal, Secret Document 21, Secret Document 22	Completing Don't Break Anything Along the Way

Reach the Goal Ring within the time limit. Pass through check points to extend your time.

Dodge the mines and the falling ice chunks.

Hit the dash panel on the breakaway bridge and pass through the first checkpoint.

Perform a Homing Attack on the aero-cannon, and then execute a Stomp to break through the ice. After passing over another breakaway bridge and through the second checkpoint, you'll have to pull off another Homing Attack/Stomp combo.

Boost over the tilting sheet of ice to make the best time. Ignore the desire to perform Homing Attacks; these baddies are electric.

Item!

An item floats in the center of the ice sheet. Pick it up before continuing on.

At the end of a long, straight corridor that contains a checkpoint, perform two Homing Attacks to reach an elevated rail. At the break in the rail, leap upward in order to pass through a red ring.

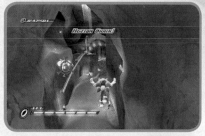

A spring marks the end of another corridor. Successfully execute three Homing Attacks to reach another high rail.

Perform a Homing Attack/Stomp combo to reach the lower path. From there, it's a leisurely run to the Goal Ring. Hit the dash panels and use Boosts to ensure you finish on time.

TIME ATTACK! RACE FOR THE GOAL!

Type	Reward(s)	Unlocked by
Daytime	Moon Medal, Secret Soundtrack 22	Item Bubble in Gaia Gate

Reach the Goal Ring within the time limit. Pass through checkpoints to extend your time.

Spagonia

USE WALL JUMPS TO GET THROUGH!

Type	Reward(s)	Unlocked by
Daytime	Moon Medal	Completing Gather the Rings at Top Speed
Use Wall Jump to bound your way up walls.		

Wall Jumps are sometimes required to reach the higher, faster path, so practice them until they come easily. Perform two Wall Jumps to reach the upper walkway and the Goal Ring.

REACH THE GOAL UNSCATHED!

Type	Reward(s)	Unlocked by
Daytime	Moon Medal, Secret Document 23	Completing Gather the Rings at Top Speed
Reach the Goal Ring in 50 seconds without taking any damage.		

The object of this mission is to dodge the attacks of the airborne menace and reach the Goal Ring in 50 seconds or less. Quick Step away from its laser-beam attack and leap over the rockets as they strike the ground.

TIP

Sonic is faster than a speeding rocket, so use boosts and leave them in your wake.

Boost to get in close, and then unleash a Homing Attack to knoc the flying fiend back. It takes two hits to tur Eggman's machine to scrap.

Item!

An item sits in the center of the road as you enter the cavern.

Time is short, so put any energy remaining in your Boost Gauge to good use.

TIME ATTACK! RACE FOR THE GOAL!

Type	Reward(s)	Unlocked by
Daytime	Moon Medal, Secret Illustration 11, Secret Document 24	Received by collecting item
Reach the Goal Ring within the time limit!		

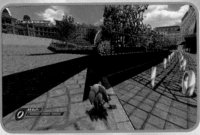

Grab the first batch rings before making sharp right turn at th entrance to the large courtyard. Take this path to the end, hitti the dash panel.

the next few dash
nels to make quick
rk of much of the
urse, flying over
e rooftops of the
vn. At the end of the
ain, turn to your left,
ke your way up the
rrow alleyway, and
:eive an item in the process. Hit the dash panel to reach
other courtyard.

Follow the path, hitting
another few dash panels
and flying through a
set of speed rings. Drift
around the tight turn
in the next courtyard,
and Lightspeed Dash
through the enemies
standing in the way.

Use the homing attack
on the next enemies,
and then Lightspeed
Dash to fly to the speed
ring that sits above a
tree-lined path. Speed
down that path through
a time-extension gate.

ntinue down
e narrow alley,
estepping to avoid
ashing into walls at
jh speed. Go through
courtyard, making a
ht turn by drifting, and
p onto the spring.

reach a zip line, use
Homing Attack on
enemies that are on
platform above the
ring. Take it down
another spring and
opel through the air
fore arriving at a
II.

e the upcoming
emies to gain access
an elevated position,
d run along the wall
t overlooks a canal.
t through a series of
ming Attack opportu-
es to pass a side-
olling area.

Head belowground
by breaking through a
group of wooden crates.
Continue forward
to reach a series of
springy poles, and leap
to new heights. Use the
speed rings to spring up
to a series of cannons.

These cannons require specific button presses to propel forward
through the air, so keep a sharp eye and a steady hand!

After landing, speed
over the ramps, hitting
the spring. Fly through
the air faster by
following the onscreen
button presses you
receive midflight. Hitting
the buttons connects
Sonic with the dash

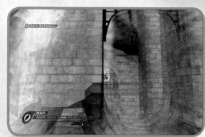

panels at the other end. Traverse the upside-down paths and
arrive at the goal.

Item!

When reaching the second 2D section, instead of
dropping down, use a Wall Jump to climb up. Do
this twice and get an item for your trouble.

GATHER RINGS AT TOP SPEED

Type	Reward(s)	Unlocked by
Daytime	Moon Medal, Secret Document 14	Item Bubble in Gaia Gate
Collect the rings		

SPECIAL MISSION! FIND THE TREASURE!

Type	Reward(s)	Unlocked by
Nighttime	Sun Medal, Secret Document 26	Item Bubble in Gaia Gate
Find the hidden treasure item!		

Head across the narrow
rooftop to claim the first
star after defeating the
enemy.

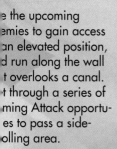

Double-jump to the roof across the way, and break the crates to the right to find the second star. Dispatch the enemies on that roof and leap to the next.

Take out the enemies on the next roof to find the third star.

Drop down and break the crates to obtain the fourth star.

Item!

From the roof, jump down to the right. Across the street, behind some pots, is an item!

Walk around the corner and find the last star behind a set of crates.

BREAK NOTHING EN ROUTE TO THE GOAL!

Type	Reward(s)	Unlocked by
Nighttime	Sun Medal, Secret Document 12	Received by collecting items
Reach the Goal Ring in 32 seconds without breaking any objects.		

This is a race against time and a test of your dashing skills. You don't have enough time to reach the Goal Ring by simply running; you'll need to dash at least a portion of the way. Start by dashing back and forth around the first several jars.

CAUTION

Any contact with a jar or crate while dashing will break it and result in failure.

Leap over the row of barrels. If necessary, u_ a double-jump to clea_ the obstacle.

If you are unsure of your complete control while dashing, resort t_ running through tight squeezes such as this one.

Item!

An item sits atop a wooden crate. You'll need to stop dashing to pick it up.

From the corner, you'll need 15 seconds to make it to the goal by running alone. If you don't have that much time, take to all fours and dash the rest of the way.

Chun-Nan

REACH THE GOAL UNSCATHED!

Type	Reward(s)	Unlocked by
Daytime	Moon Medal, Secret Document 25	Completing Don't Break Anything Along the Way

Reach the goal within 2'50, without taking damage.

Once the paved road ends, turrets pop out of the ground, looking to prematurely end your run at the goal. Don't approach them head-on and you'll avoid their bullets. When you get close, use Homing Attacks to destroy them.

In the cave, leap over this single row of spiked balls.

Stick to the middle of the road to hit dash panels and avoid the large, spiked balls.

After a spring throws you into the air, perform three Homing Attacks to reach a small outcropping and destroy the red fan.

Leap off the first outcropping and execute two more Homing Attacks to reach the second outcropping and destroy the fan perched upon it. Repeat the process to reach the third and fourth rocky platforms.

Item!

Take a brief respite from your aerial acrobatics and grab the item that sits upon the fourth outcropping.

Hit the spring and perform a midair dash to get through the rainbow ring, which will propel you to the faraway road. Once your feet hit the ground, boost to the Goal Ring.

GATHER RINGS AT TOP SPEED!

Type	Reward(s)	Unlocked by
Daytime	Moon Medal, Secret Document 27	Item Bubble in Gaia Gate

Collect 100 rings!

Race down the narrow path collecting rings along the way. Hit the spring, and Lightspeed Dash at the peak to obtain the rings suspended in midair.

Hit the elevated spring to propel across the stage. Follow the onscreen button presses that appear to launch off the last four springs. Missing these buttons seals Sonic's fate in the water below.

Go through a couple of rooms containing enemies. Lightspeed Dash through them while avoiding the lifte areas that attempt to block Sonic's progress.

Hit the ground running and collect the remaining rings needed to complete the stage.

Continue down the path, crossing time-extension gates along the way. Take the path around the water to secure a quicker time.

Item!

Keep Sonic from gathering too many rings at the start, and there is an item waiting for you after the long action chain near the end.

Push forward, spiraling through the course's upside-down pathways and ramps. Follow the onscreen action buttons at the spring. Wall-climb to a walkway that leads to a grind rail that takes you to more ramps.

TIME ATTACK! RACE FOR THE GOAL!

Type	Reward(s)	Unlocked by
Daytime	Moon Medal	Item Bubble in Gaia Gate
Reach the Goal Ring within the time limit!		

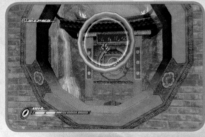

Race ahead, making sure to land on as mar dash panels as possibl Launch forward off one of the dash panels and through a series o speed rings. Continue running on the other side.

Hit the first set of dash panels to pick up speed, and use a Homing Attack on the enemies waiting at the end of the body of water. After dismantling the enemies, Lightspeed Dash down the walkway and onto the spring. Use a Homing Attack on the enemies in the air to make it through the speed ring, which launches Sonic to the next area.

Be careful to jump over the upcoming steps. You don't want Sonic to trip and slow down! Cross the time-extension gate and step onto the dash panel to quickly move forward.

TIME ATTACK! RACE FOR THE GOAL!

Type	Reward(s)	Unlocked by
Daytime	Moon Medal, Secret Illustration 42	Recaived from collecting items
Reach the Goal Ring within the time limit!		

Race down the confined walkway, launching off the spring at the end. Use a Homing Attack off the jump, rush the upcoming enemies, and then traverse the open area.

Hop from spring to spring over the water; follow the onscreen action buttons on the last few to make it across.

Traverse the course, breaking any jars on the path to collect health. Atop a group of ledges, another set of enemies appears. Eliminate them using well-placed combos.

...down the path and ...a Homing Attack ...series of enemies ...appear. Lightspeed ...into a line of rings ...each a speed ring.

Defeat all the enemies to claim the Goal Ring at the end of the long walkway.

...forward and ...the next couple of ...panels, looking ...for a cannon that ...ires you follow the ...reen action buttons. ...going, avoiding ...enemies that fire ...ectiles.

BATTLE ROYALE! TAKE DOWN ALL COMERS!

Type	Reward(s)	Unlocked by
Nighttime	Sun Medal, Secret Document 27	Item Bubble in Gaia Gate
Defeat the entire horde of enemies!		

Run down the path and follow the onscreen button presses that appear while you're in midair. Next, follow along the dash panels that propel Sonic toward the finish.

Traverse the level, hopping up the platforms while defeating the throngs of enemies. After defeating the final two foes, you complete the stage and Sonic is victorious.

REACH THE GOAL RING WITHOUT GETTING HIT!

Type	Reward(s)	Unlocked by
...httime	Sun Medal, Secret Illustration 1	Item Bubble in Gaia Gate
...h the goal with only a small amount of health!		

Use the glowing ledge to reach the elevated level, and defeat the nearby enemies. Use combo attacks to minimize damage against Sonic.

Shamar

GATHER RINGS AT TOP SPEED!

Type	Reward(s)	Unlocked by
Daytime	Moon Medal, Secret Document 28	Item Bubble in Gaia Gate
Collect 150 Rings		

Step into the buggy and cruise through the desert.

Look out for the pillars and pop-up obstacles that appear throughout the course.

Use the dash panels to send Sonic on a straight path toward large numbers of rings.

Item!

Fall off of the second cliff to the left to find an item!

TIME ATTACK! RACE FOR THE GOAL!

Type	Reward(s)	Unlocked by
Daytime	Moon Medal, Secret Document 29	Item Bubble in Gaia Gate
Reach the Goal Ring within the time limit!		

Item!

At the start, keep veering to the right into two sets of boxes. If you're lucky, you'll hit a spring, sending you to a secret area with an item!

Hop into the buggy and crash through the enemies that lie in the path. Bust through the crates on the right-side path to reach a time-extension gate.

Take another right when the ground drops out from under Sonic, and you reach a time-extension gate. Use the dash panels to avoid falling into a large canyon. Cross another gate before exiting the craft to take the course on foot.

Hit a dash panel and Sonic is off to the rac— The panels do most of the work, with only a Lightspeed Dash nee— here and there to fur— your progress.

Arrive at another bu— and hop in to manag— the desert floor, whe— stone pillars impede your path.

Don't be afraid to crash through some jars to reach your destination. Dismount the vehicle and run to the goal to finish the course.

SONIC UNLEASHED™

SPECIAL MISSION! FIND THE TREASURE!

Type	Reward(s)	Unlocked by
...httime	Sun Medal, Secret Document 18	Item Bubble in Gaia Gate
...the hidden treasure item!		

Defeat the enemies that appear once Sonic moves forward into the stage to find the first star.

Grab the second star on the crates that lie atop the rearmost elevated platform.

Item!

...the second area, break the jars under the ...verhang to the right. There is an item inside one ...them.

...tinue forward and ...he stairs. Destroy the ...in the far left corner ...laim the third star.

...eat the enemies in ...next area to obtain ...number four.

Destroy the crates in the corner next to the glowing exit to find the fifth star.

BREAK NOTHING EN ROUTE TO THE GOAL!

Type	Reward(s)	Unlocked by
Nighttime	Sun Medal, Secret Document 31	Item Bubble in Gaia Gate
Reach the Goal Ring without breaking anything!		

Take the crate that starts in the center and place it on each of the blue buttons around the room. While the crate is on the button, press the green button inside the door, which opens to give you access to the Goal Ring.

Item!

After pressing all of the buttons, wait several seconds after the door with the Goal Ring opens, and then the last door will swing open, allowing you to grab an item.

Adabat

TIME ATTACK! RACE FOR THE GOAL!

Type	Reward(s)	Unlocked by
Daytime	Moon Medal, Secret Document 15	Completing the Egg Lancer boss
Reach the goal within the time limit!		

Quickly dodge to avo[id] the jars on the first stretch. Keep a wary eye on the robot that attacks throughout th[e] stage.

Run along the narrow walkway, avoiding the falling tribal-head statues. Hit the spring and Lightspeed Dash across the gap. On the other side, use another spring to reach a hanging bar. Use the bar to swing to the nearby platform.

When the robot attacks, get as far away from any jars in the vicinity as quickly as possible; a dash in the wrong direction spells certain doom for the blue hedgehog.

Avoid the tribal heads again, maneuvering through them while being cautious to not fall off the side of the narrow lane. Run to the spring and fly into the cannon. The cannon fires Sonic across the stage; follow the onscreen button presses to land in a better location.

REACH THE GOAL UNSCATHED!

Type	Reward(s)	Unlocked by
Daytime	Moon Medal, Secret Movie 36	Finding every item other tha[n] Secret Movie 36
Reach the Goal Ring without taking damage!		

Look out for the falling tribal heads in the cavern by sticking to the center of the walkway. Take the tight turn that appears before running straight to victory.

Hit the first curve carefully to avoid fall[ing] into the pit.

DON'T BREAK ANYTHING ALONG THE WAY!

Type	Reward(s)	Unlocked by
Daytime	Moon Medal, Secret Document 30	Item Bubble in Gaia Gate
Reach the Goal Ring, dodging the jars as you go!		

Maneuver the windin[g] paths, looking out for the exploding bombs that drop from the sk[y]

... the Lightspeed Dash
...spatch enemies and
...ch over the chasm
... extreme speed to
...ch the Goal Ring.

Double-jump over the
spike balls entrenched
in the ground. Break
through the jars and
containers that sit on the
narrow walkway.

GATHER RINGS AT TOP SPEED!

Type	Reward(s)	Unlocked by
...aytime	Moon Medal	Item Bubble in Gaia Gate
...ect 150 rings!		

Leap from glowing
pole to glowing pole to
reach the other side of
the large gap. Carefully
maneuver down the
narrow walkways high
above the jungle.

Collect the rings along
the path, nabbing some
easy ones any time a
dash panel sends Sonic
careening in a certain
direction.

Use the glowing ledge
to hoist up to the next
level, but hop off when
you see a break in the
spike balls.

Use the Lightspeed
Dash to propel forward
whenever a set of rings
lies over a deep chasm.

Slowly and steadily
continue down the
narrow paths. Break
any jars that stand in
the way, and reach the
Goal Ring at the end of
a final narrow walkway.

...ying in the course's
...ter keeps Sonic safe
...n those falling tribal
...ds.

Item!

Just past the Goal Ring is an item on a platform. Be
careful not to touch the ring if you want to get it.

BATTLE ROYALE! TAKE ON ALL COMERS!

Type	Reward(s)	Unlocked by
Nighttime	Sun Medal, Secret Illustration 43	Item Bubble in Gaia Gate
Defeat the entire horde of enemies!		

REACH THE GOAL RING WITHOUT GETTING HIT!

Type	Reward(s)	Unlocked by
...ghttime	Sun Medal, Secret Document 19	Item Bubble in Gaia Gate
...ach the goal with only a small amount of health!		

Eggmanland

REACH THE GOAL UNSCATHED!

Type	Reward(s)	Unlocked by
Daytime	Moon Medal, Secret Document 35	Completing Time Attack! Race for the Goal!

Reach the Goal Ring without taking damage!

Hit the ground running, and use a Homing Attack on the rocket-firing enemies on the path's upper level.

Follow the path the dash panels make, stopping only to use a Homing Attack on the enemies standing in the way.

Follow the onscreen commands precisely to reach an upper level, and perform a wall-jump to continue down that path.

Hop onto the rocket and avoid the floating spike balls by flying through them. Soon after the spikes, the rocket throws Sonic off. Skate down the new path and race forward to collect the prize.

SPECIAL MISSION! FIND THE TREASURE!

Type	Reward(s)	Unlocked by
Nighttime	Sun Medal, Secret Document 33	Item Bubble in Gaia Gate

Find the hidden treasure item!

Grab on to the pole above to reach the fi star atop the moving blocks. Hop off the block and out of the area the block pushe into.

Press the green button on the elevated platform in the next area to unleash three enemies. Defeat them to claim the second star.

Item!

There is an item on a high ledge above the Thunde Bats in the same location as Eggmanland Act III

Break the crates on th main platform below grab the third star.

Lift the door to reach the next area, then open both of the doors in that hallway. Enter the first door and break open the crates on the right to collect star number four.

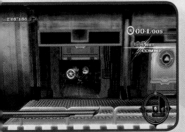

Enter the other door to reach a series of catwalks. At the end of these lies the fifth star.

REACH THE GOAL RING WITHOUT GETTING HIT!

Type	Reward(s)	Unlocked by
Nighttime	Sun Medal, Secret Document 34	Item Bubble in Gaia Gate
Reach the goal with only a small amount of health!		

Item!

Sprint across from the entrance to the elevator before it drops below.

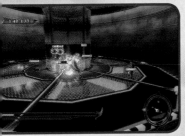

Enter the descending elevator and defeat the enemies there by using high-damage combos.

To reach the Goal Ring at the bottom, survive the descent by picking up the health that enemies release.

BATTLE ROYALE! TAKE ON ALL COMERS!

Type	Reward(s)	Unlocked by
Nighttime	Sun Medal, Secret Document 36	Item Bubble in Gaia Gate
Defeat the entire horde of enemies!		

Item!

If you head towards the camera, you will get an item.

Leap over to the dome structure to begin battle.

Take the enemies out en masse by using combos and the Were-Wallop.

Wave after wave of enemies attacks Sonic's position until all 100 are defeated.

APPENDIX: GAIA GATE DOORS
Apotos

DOOR ONE

Item!

Grab the third item after you reach the other side of the treadmill.

Required Medals

Sun	Moon	Rewards
14	14	Secret Soundtrack 4, 31, 47

Item!

Climb the glowing pole and leap across the chasm to the ledge beyond. Climb up and claim the first of three items in this area.

DOOR TWO

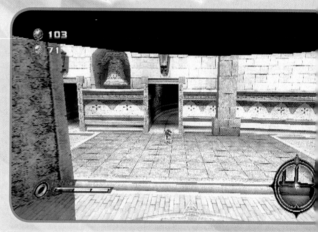

Required Medals

Sun	Moon	Rewards
43	45	Secret Illustration 96, Secret Mission

Item!

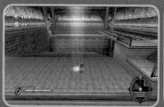 

Stand in the beam of sunlight to revert to Hedgehog form. Run down the center of the treadmill and leap to reach the floating item.

Climb up to the glowing ledge to the entrance's left. Continue forward along the elevated path to reach two glowing poles. Swing from pole to pole to reach the walkway on the other side.

Activate the lever on the walkway's right side to turn on a moving platform. Leap onto the moving platform and ride it under the beam of sunlight to change back into Hedgehog form.

Use the shaft of sunlight to revert to Hedgehog form and cross the first treadmill.

nce in Hedgehog rm, leap from the oving platform onto e elevated ledge to e treadmill's right, nd step on the button open the door elow. Quickly leap own to the treadmill hile still in Hedgehog form and race into the now-open om.

Item!

Grab the item at the end of the first treadmill.

Item!

Move across another treadmill, take a right, and then ride the moving platform up to the roof of the small structure to grab the second item.

After you revert to Werehog form, grab the glowing ledge, pull yourself up, and nab the last item in the area.

DOOR THREE

Required Medals

Sun	Moon	Rewards
33	26	1-Up Item x2, Secret Soundtrack 12

Now in Werehog form, use the glowing, horizontal poles to reach a small platform. Step on the green button to raise the distant door.

ames.com

Mazuri

DOOR ONE

Descend the stairs, grab the metal crate, and place it at the bottom of the elevated platform at the walkway's end. Climb onto the metal crate to reach the elevated platform, where there is a ray of sunlight that reverts Sonic back into Hedgehog form.

Hop onto the nearby platform and use Sonic's Lightspeed Dash to reach the platform on the other side.

Required Medals

Sun	Moon	Rewards
87	69	Secret Soundtrack 29, 1-Up x2

Break through the destructible stone door on the left to access the room behind it.

Continue to the other destructible stone door and tear it down. Follow the winding hallway and use the glowing poles to swing to the other side of a chasm; then climb up to the glowing edge on the chasm's other side.

DOOR TWO

Required Medals

Sun	Moon	Rewards
55	46	Secret Mission x3

t the door on the
ght to access the
om behind it. Exit the
om and shinny up
e glowing pole. From
e pole, hop onto
e nearby platform
d shinny down the
owing pole at its
d.

Grab the metal crate
at the bottom of the
glowing pole and
place it up against the
grate on the chamber's
other side. Hop
down into the ray of
sunlight and revert into
Hedgehog form. Climb

onto the metal crate and crawl through the small space
nder the metal fencing.

Follow the path
behind the crate while
grabbing the rings to
reach the end of this
area.

DOOR THREE

Required Medals

Sun	Moon	Rewards
14	15	1-Up Item, Secret Illustration 63, 95

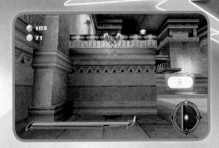

Simply grab the
glowing ledge, pull
yourself up, and take
the item!

Leap from one moving
platform to the next,
working your way to
the room's right side.
Leap from the last
platform to the top of a
structure.

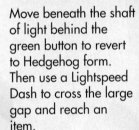

Step on the green
button and a small
platform near the
partially opened gate
will begin moving up
and down.

Move beneath the shaft
of light behind the
green button to revert
to Hedgehog form.
Then use a Lightspeed
Dash to cross the large
gap and reach an
item.

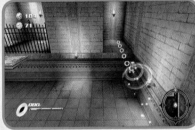

Once the rings reappear, use another Lightspeed Dash to
return to the platform with the green button. Wait until you
transform back into a Werehog and use the light to once
again revert to Hedgehog form. Quickly hop down from the
platform and make your way to the opposite corner of the
room. Jump onto the small platform and ride it up to the high
walkway. Then, crawl beneath the partially opened gate and
collect the item on the other side.

Spagonia

DOOR ONE

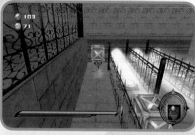

Drop to the floor and run down the first aisle. Grab the iron crate and carry it back to the top of the aisle. Throw it in front of the first beam of light.

Required Medals		
Sun	Moon	Rewards
23	15	Secret Mission 1, 3, 1-Up Item, Secret Soundtrack 6

Item!

You're now able to grab the item hovering over the blue button.

Item!

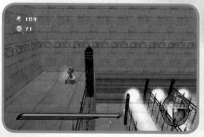

The first item is at the end of the left ledge.

Now, grab the second iron crate from aisle two and throw it in front of the second beam of light. This frees up the third crate.

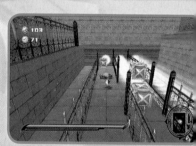

The only way you can reach the other three items is in Werehog form. However, if you come in contact with the beams of light, you'll instantly revert to Hedgehog form. You must manipulate the iron crates to both block the light and to facilitate access to the two other items.

Grab the third iron crate and drop it at the end of aisle four. It will block the light, allowing you to hop on and double-jump up to the high ledge.

Item!

Three down and one to go!

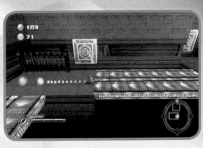

p back down and
k up the crate you
ed to reach the
cond item. Drop it on
e blue button in aisle
o. This reverses the
admill's direction,
owing a Werehog to
vel upon it.

Required Medals		
Sun	**Moon**	**Rewards**
95	69	Secret Soundtrack 25, Secret Movie 24, 30, 34

Walk into the sunbeam
and transform into
Hedgehog form to be
able to traverse the two
treadmill walkways.
On the other side of
those lies a destructible
stone door; break it
down once back in
Werehog form.

From the top of aisle
one, grab the first crate
and walk it down the
aisle to the end of aisle
four. Throw it onto the
treadmill and watch it
travel all the way up,
blocking the beam of
light.

Behind the stone door
lies a floating bomb;
take it out of the
chamber, down one
treadmill, and throw
it toward the stone
door at the end of that
treadmill to open a
new room. Step on the

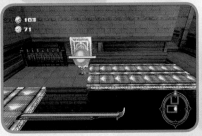

button inside that room to activate a moving platform near
the area's entrance.

Head over to the
moving platform
and take it up to the
elevated walkway.

Item!

Use the iron
crate to reach
the fourth and
final item in
the area.

DOOR THREE

DOOR TWO

Required Medals		
Sun	**Moon**	**Rewards**
72	52	Secret Mission x2, Secret Art 96

While in Werehog form, move onto the first moving platform. Next, walk onto the stone pillar and into the shaft of light, reverting to Hedgehog form. While in this form, move onto the

platform on the right, then crouch down and ride it under the upper walkway.

Item!

The first item is just past the upper walkway, hovering over the nearby moving platform.

To reach the next item, take the latest moving platform to the back corner of the room and revert to Hedgehog form in the shaft of light. Step onto the platform, moving back under the upper

walkway. Make sure you crouch! You don't want to end up falling to your doom. Back on the other side, transfer to the platform moving up to the walkway. Jump onto the walkway.

Item!

The second item is resting on the upper walkway.

While in Werehog form, jump onto the glowing pole and slide down to the shaft of light, turning back into Hedgehog form. Quickly hop onto the nearby moving

platform and crouch to avoid being knocked down by the oncoming pillar. Once the platform clears the obstacle, it starts toward the pillar in the room's corner.

Item!

The third and last item is on the pillar in the corner.

Hop back onto the last platform and ride it until it turns back toward the glowing pole. Just before it turns, jump off the platform and land on the walkway below. Navigate back to the entrance and you're home free!

DOOR FOUR

Required Medals

Sun	Moon	Rewards
93	69	Secret Soundtrack 27, Secret Movie 22

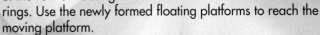

Throw the floating bomb into the destructible stone door and hop into the chamber that opens up. Run down that hallway and into the sunbeam, reverting into Hedgehog form.

Return to the nearest sunbeam to revert Sonic into Hedgehog form. Get back onto the floating platform and use the Lightspeed Dash to reach the chamber at the end of the row of floating rings. Use the newly formed floating platforms to reach the moving platform.

e a Lightspeed sh to zip from tform to platform. Sonic transform Werehog form d grab the floating mb. Step onto the pended platform d it activates, owing Sonic to throw the floating bomb at the destructible ne door at the end of the floating platform's circuit.

Take the floating platform to the chamber Sonic opened earlier with the bomb. Hop onto the floating platform inside to reach the other side. Open the door and exit back out to the area's entrance.

131

Chun-nan

DOOR ONE

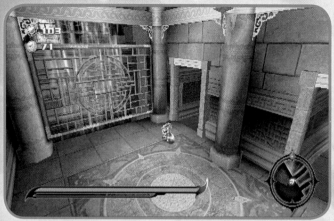

Hop up a few large stairs to grab the second item in the area. Continue up th stairs and walk arou the path to a small gap. Hop over the g to claim the third an final item.

Required Medals

Sun	Moon	Rewards
33	21	1-Up Item, Secret Soundtrack 11, 48

Smash the breakable door and enter the shaft of light. As a Hedgehog, traverse the fast-moving treadmill. On the other side, wait until you revert to Werehog form, and smash open the first breakable door to reach the item beyond.

DOOR TWO

Required Medals

Sun	Moon	Rewards
33	34	Secret Soundtrack 18, 20, 26, 1-Up Item

Destroy the other breakable door and then lift the ornate door. Use the shaft of light to transform into a Hedgehog; then run through the last breakable door and over the treadmill that sits behind it.

Climb up the pole ar leap to the nearby platform. Grab the item and then stand beneath the shaft of light to transform int a Hedgehog.

Use a Lightspeed Dash to reach the far walkway. Another item is yours for the taking.

Walk around the platform and pick up the floating bomb. Drop to the lower walkway and hurl the bomb at the stone door. A direct hit destroys the door, allowing you to reach the path beyond via a double-jump.

Grab the item and step on the green button to activate the moving platform located near the entrance.

Hop onto the moving platform to reach the high ledge and grab the final item.

DOOR THREE

Required Medals

Sun	Moon	Rewards
86	60	Secret Soundtrack 7, Secret Mission, 1-Up Item

Step into the sunbeam and revert to Hedgehog form to travel down the treadmill. Step on the button on the other side to open the ornate door near the entrance. Grab the metal crate near the button. Take it into the newly accessible area to use as a step to reach the elevated walkway.

Step into the sunbeam to revert to Hedgehog form, and use a Lightspeed Dash to reach the platform across the way. Climb up onto the glowing ledge to reach the platform above.

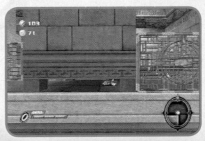

Drop back down onto the previous level, get back to the sunbeam across the way to revert to Hedgehog form, and Lightspeed Dash back across. Crawl under the large structure; once Sonic reaches the other side, Lightspeed Dash over the treadmill to the ledge on the other side.

DOOR FOUR

On the other side of the gap, shinny up the glowing pole in Werehog form. Hop onto the adjacent walkway and pick up the metal crate at the other end. Take the crate down to the button directly below and place it on the button, which activates a nearby lift.

Take the lift up to the next platform and use the sunbeam to revert to Hedgehog form. Utilize the Lightspeed Dash to cross the large crevasse.

Required Medals		
Sun	Moon	Rewards
89	69	Secret Soundtrack 28, Secret Movie 28, 29

Run over to the horizontal pole and use it to swing across the chasm. Turn the corner and enter a small crevice to reach a sunbeam at the walkway's end. Revert to Hedgehog form and exit out to the main zone, using a Lightspeed Dash to cross the large gap.

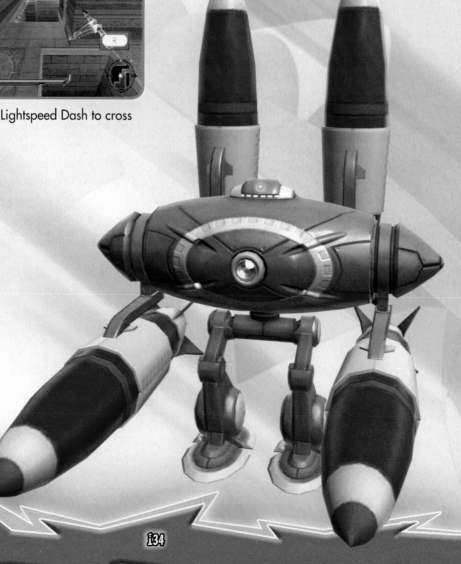

Holoska

DOOR ONE

Continue down the walkway and use the now-moving floating platform to reach the isolated dais on the other side.

Required Medals

Sun	Moon	Rewards
60	46	1-Up Item, Secret Soundtrack 15, 17

DOOR TWO

Step into the the sunbeam, revert to Hedgehog form, and Lightspeed Dash across the large chasm. Follow the winding corridors to reach an apparent dead end. Turn around, open the

ornate door, and enter the newly accessible chamber. Return to the dead end, climb up to the glowing ledge, grab the metal crate, and place it on the button below. This activates a moving platform in another location of the area.

Required Medals

Sun	Moon	Rewards
23	21	Secret Soundtrack 5, 14

Item!

The first item sits behind the iron crate, just to the right of the room's entrance.

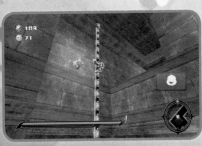

Step back into the sunbeam and Lightspeed Dash back across the chasm. Once Sonic has transformed into Werehog form again, climb the glowing pole, hop onto the elevated platform to the left, then use the pole to propel Sonic onto the platform on the right.

The ornate door can only be lifted from the other side. Step into the shaft of light and revert to Hedgehog form. Run over the treadmill, turn right, and lift the door (after you've returned to Werehog form).

Go back and get the iron crate, but travel over the treadmill to avoid the light. Lift the iron crate and walk it through the door. The crate blocks the sun and keeps Sonic from transforming into a Hedgehog. Place the crate at the base of the high structure and use it to reach the top.

Item!

The iron crate allows you to reach this high ledge and grab the concealed item.

Item!

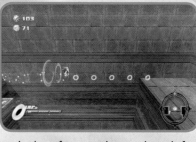

Use your arms to reach the glowing ledge. Pull yourself up and this item is yours.

DOOR THREE

Required Medals

Sun	Moon	Rewards
90	69	Secret Soundtract 24, Secret Mission, Secret Movie 23, 25

Hoist Sonic up to the glowing ledge, hop over to the sunbeam, and revert to Hedgehog form. Make your way from platform to platform, quickly stepping on the button to open the ornate door below to reach the row of rings. Use a Lightspeed Dash to cross the large gap before Sonic turns back into a Werehog.

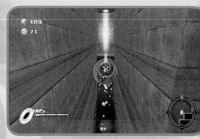

Step into the sunbeam to revert to Hedgehog form, and use a Lightspeed Dash to return to the main area. Climb back up to the upper level using the glowing ledge, and hop over to the other side using the moving floating platform to reach an isolated area in the left corner.

Enter the ornate door Sonic opened earlier, hop onto the floating platform, and hit the button on the other side to start it moving. Use it to reach the moving lift, and step into the sunbeam to revert to Hedgehog form. Lightspeed Dash from platform to platform to reach the final one above the button in that room.

Shamar

DOOR ONE

Grab one of the crates and place it over one of the jets of fire to gain access to the area behind the wall of flame.

Required Medals

Sun	Moon	Rewards
70	59	Secret Illustration 89, Secret Soundtrack 21, Secret Mission

Hoist Sonic up onto the platform lined with the glowing edge. Step into the sunbeam on the platform to revert back into Hedgehog form. Use it to race down the nearby treadmill and over to the metal crate on the platform at its end. Grab the crate once Sonic has transformed into Werehog form and take it back down the treadmill.

Take the crate over to the elevated platform in the nearby corner and place it adjacent to the platform. Run over to the metal crate around the corner and grab it. Bring it over to the first crate and place it on top of it. Hop up to the elevated platform.

DOOR TWO

Required Medals

Sun	Moon	Rewards
68	56	Secret Illustration 5, 40, Secret Mission

Hop up onto the elevated walkway and turn the crank until the floating platform is positioned adjacent to the caged area.

Run over to the horizontal poles and use them to swing across the gap. Swing from the upcoming horizontal poles to reach the platform with the sunbeam glaring down on it. Step into

Required Medals		
Sun	Moon	Rewards
96	69	Secret Movie 27, 32, 1-Up Item

the sunbeam and revert to Hedgehog form. Use a Lightspeed Dash to reach the caged enclosure, grab the metal crate in the cage, and place it on the platform that was moved earlier.

Run back to the crank and turn it so that the moving platform is positioned next to the blue button. Swing over to the button and place the crate onto it to weigh it down.

Use the horizontal glowing poles to reac the area on the other side. Step into the sunbeam to revert inta Hedgehog form and quickly crawl under th crevice indicated by the rings next to it. Ru over to the treadmill and traverse it before transforming bac into Werehog form. Hop onto the elevated platform, then hop back down to grab the metal crate and send it down th treadmill. Place it onto the blue button to start the elevator near the sunbeam. Take the platform up to grab the metal crate and place it on the other ornate platform.

Run back to the crank yet again and turn it so that the moving platform is positioned in between the walkway and the elevated platform. Hop over to the isolated platform.

Step into the sunbeam again to revert to Hedgehog form, and speed down the treadmill to the chamber's far side to reach the crate on the other side. Grab it once Sonic has turned back into a Werehog, and send it down the treadmill. Take to the nearby button and place it atop to activate a floating platform near the first one Sonic activated.

DOOR THREE

Hop onto the moving platform, grab the crate, and take it across to the walkway on the other side. Place the crate on the button to activate a moving platform in the first chamber.

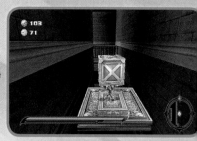

SONIC UNLEASHED™

DOOR FOUR

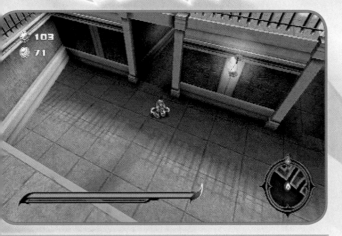

has changed back into the Werehog, use the glowing pole to climb up the next level. Grab the metal crate and take it over to the flame jets to block the lowest of them. Go back to the sunbeam and revert to Hedgehog form. Lightspeed Dash using the nearby rings to reach the other side. Once there, grab the metal crates and throw them down to lower level.

Place the crates that are now on the lower level atop two of the flame jets, and grab the nearby metal crate. Place it over the last flame jet and head back over to the horizontal flame jets from earlier.

Required Medals

Sun	Moon	Rewards
43	52	Secret Soundtrack 30, Secret Mission x3

Head past the horizontal flame jets and Lightspeed Dash to where the vertical jets once were to reach the walkway on the other side.

Race over to the sunbeam near the jets of flame, revert to Hedgehog form, and run back to the first area; Lightspeed Dash across the large chasm. Once Sonic

Adabat

DOOR ONE

Required Medals

Sun	Moon	Rewards
80	69	Secret Illustration 61, Secret Mission x2

Step onto the moving platform at the entrance, and take it to the walkway across the gap. Continue down that way and step onto the moving platform that takes Sonic to a stationary platform in a corner. Take the next moving platform to a fenced-off platform, then take yet another moving platform to a fenced-off walkway. Press the green button at the walkway's end to activate a moving platform elsewhere in the area.

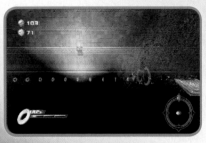

Head back to the first walkway Sonic arrived at that contained a moving platform and take the one you didn't take previously. Follow the path the floating platform creates, and

step into the sunbeam. Use the Lightspeed Dash to cross the large chasm and reach the platform on the other side. Climb up to the glowing ledge once Sonic has changed back into the Werehog, and take the moving platform to the next platform.

Head back to the entrance and take the alternate platform that is now moving due to the switch being activated. Take that platform to the next moving platform and arrive at the isolated platform at the walkway's end.

DOOR TWO

Required Medals

Sun	Moon	Rewards
97	69	Secret Movie 31, 33, 35, Secret Soundtrack 23

Take the treadmills to the end of the line, where a metal crate awaits. Place the crate on the nearby blue button, step into the sunbeam, and get back onto the treadmill as a Hedgehog.

Quickly head back to the entrance and take the treadmill into a secluded area. Place the metal crate you find there on a button that activates a floating platform.

Get on the floating platform and take it to the upper level. Grab the metal crate and throw it down to the area between the two treadmills. Hop down and place the crate on the blue button activate a floating platform, then get onto the moving tform nearby. Head over the fenced-in area to reach an vated walkway, take the moving platform over to another rby walkway, and place on the button the metal crate t you find there. Head back to the treadmills, over to the ere the sunbeam is breaking through.

ce back in the beam chamber, nge to Werehog m and get on the ving platform to ess the walkway ve.

Take the path and follow it around the chamber, up a set of stairs, and across a gap where a sunbeam beats down. Activate the lever to turn off the flame jets and step into the sunbeam to revert to Hedgehog form. Quickly run toward the row of rings, and use a Lightspeed Dash to reach an isolated platform. Head back to the platform with the sunbeam, and use it to switch into Werehog form yet again.

Move the lever again to turn off the flames, but this time get on the moving platform afterward. Take the moving platform over to the landing on the other side.

Once again, head back to the sunbeam platform, flip the switch, and quickly hop down to the lower level to access an area that was once hidden by flames. Once inside, activate the lever.

DOOR THREE

Required Medals

un	Moon	Rewards
0	60	Secret Illustration 92, Secret Mission x3

DOOR FOUR

nearby moving platform. Get back on the moving platform with the sunbeam, and Lightspeed Dash across the area to reach the elevated platform, now with an activated moving platform working next to it.

Take that moving platform to another ledge with an ornate door on it. Pry open the ornate door to reach the other side.

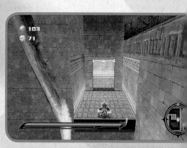

Sun	Moon	Rewards
99	69	Secret Soundtrack 3, 16, 1-Up Item, Secret Mission

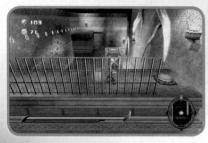

Step into the sunbeam to change into Hedgehog form, then race down the treadmill to grab a metal crate. Send the metal crate careening down the treadmill and follow it. Grab it once Sonic has switched back into the Werehog form, and block the nearby jets by carrying it through the flames. Place the crate atop the button on the other side to activate a moving platform. Head over to the moving platform and step into the sunbeam to turn into Hedgehog form. Once at the top, use a Lightspeed Dash to send Sonic spiraling across the entire area over to a platform.

Drop off the platform, grab the nearby metal crate, and place it on the button that lies at the top of a graded walkway to activate the